AF552824

PSYCHOLOGY AND CURRICULUM

BOOKS BY THE SAME AUTHORS

Published by Discovery Publishing House
New Delhi

Science Curriculum

Elementary Curriculum

Language Arts Curriculum

Philosophy and Curriculum

Psychology and Curriculum

Improving School Administration

Modern Elementary School

Teaching English Successfully

Teaching Science Successfully

Teaching Mathematics Successfully

Teaching Social Studies Successfully

Teaching Reading Successfully

Teaching Language Arts Successfully

Teaching Science in Elementary Schools

Teaching Mathematics in Elementary Schools

Teaching Social Studies in Elementary Schools

PSYCHOLOGY AND CURRICULUM

By

Dr. Marlow Ediger

Professor Emeritur in Education
Truman State University
201 W. 22nd. Box 417
North Newton KS-67117
United States of America

Dr. Digumarti Bhaskara Rao

M.Sc., M.A., M.A., M.Ed., Ph.D.
R.V.R. College of Education
D–43, Srinivasa, Nagar
Guntur—2522006
Andhra Pradesh
(India)

DISCOVERY PUBLISHING HOUSE
NEW DELHI

Published by:
Namit Wasan
DISCOVERY PUBLISHING HOUSE PVT. LTD.
4383/4B, Ansari Road, Darya Ganj
New Delhi-110 002 (India)
Phone : +91-11-23279245; 23253475; 43596065
E-mail : discoverybooksindia@gmail.com
discoverypublishinghouse@gmail.com
namitwasan9@gmail.com
web : www.discoverypublishinggroup.com

Edition: **2020**

ISBN: 978-81-7141-691-2

Psychology and Curriculum

© **Authors** (2003)

All rights reserved. No part of this publication should be reproduced, stored in a retrieval system, or transmitted in any form or by any means: electronic, mechanical, photocopying, recording or otherwise, without the prior written permission of the author and the publisher.

This book has been published in good faith that the material provided by authors/editors is original. Every effort is made to ensure accuracy of material, but the publisher and printer will not be held responsible for any inadvertent error(s). In case of any dispute, all legal matters are to be settled under Delhi jurisdiction only.

Printed at:
Infinity Imaging Systems
Delhi

Dedicated
to the World Famous Educationist

DR. LAVU RATHAIAH

M.Sc., M.Ed., D.J., Ph.D.

Founder, Chairman, Managing Director and Correspondent
Vignan Family of Educational Institutions
Educating about twenty thousand students
Vignan Engineering College
Vignan Institute of Information Technology
Vignan Institute of Science and Technology
Vignan School of Post-graduate Studies
Vignan Degree College
Vignan Junior Colleges
Vignan Vidyalayas Junior Colleges
Vignan Co-operative Junior Colleges
Vignan Day-Scholars Junior Colleges
Vignan Prabhodananda Prasanthi Niketan Suprabhatham
Vignan Vidyalayas
Vignan High Schools
Vignan Publishers

Preface

Psychology and Education are the two sides of the same coin and are interwoven inseparably. As one of the major player in educational enterprise, the Psychology influences the curriculum to a large extent. Considering the inter-relationship between Psychology and Curriculum, this book on "Psychology and Curriculum" is written to provide pre-service and in-service teachers an opportunity to study and appraise diverse schools of thought in determining objectives, learning experiences, evaluation procedures, etc. We tried to make the content as practical and utilitarian as possible. We strongly believe that educators and teachers need to possess a strong framework from which the curriculum for pupils may be envisioned and brought forth. Psychology in a practical subject which has its many applications in curriculum development. We hope the curriculum designers along with practising and preservice teachers may use the ideas of this book in developing and implementing the best curriculum possible.

Marlow Ediger
Digumarti Bhaskara Rao

Contents

The Psychology and Philosophy of Education

The psychology of instruction is important for teachers and school administrators to use in assisting pupils to achieve more optimally in the classroom setting as well as achieve well later on in life's endeavours. Life in society continues to become increasingly complex. More formal schooling is needed by pupils to do well in a technological world. Tasks formerly performed by manual labour and by machines is being done via computers. The informational world certainly is here. This should aided in making better decisions. But not all can afford in the home setting to have computers and other technology. Schools differ too from area to area as to how much technology is available. Technology is expensive in that computers become outdated, cause problems, cost money and work to keep them operating, and might be difficult to operate.

One thing is certain, pupils do need the best education possible to live and work in a world of complexity. Thus, the teacher needs to use appropriate principles of learning to assist pupils to do well in school. These principles of learning are indeed excellent and might be difficult to implement on the part of selected pupils. However, as much effort as is necessary must be used in their implementation. It is important to help pupils learn as much as possible.

Principals of Learning from Educational Psychology

Teachers when teaching have accepted selected standards to use in teaching pupils. Thus, there are certain standards which are used and others which are frowned upon. Research has indicated what is good and should be stressed in ongoing lessons and units of study. Other standards will be based upon a system of beliefs or a philosophy of instruction. Moral and ethical standards also enter in to the picture of teaching and learning. What might be selected guidelines, when used in teaching and learning, may assist pupils to achieve more optimally?

ENGAGEMENT IN LEARNING

The teacher needs to engage pupils in learning. To engage pupils in learning involves active involvement mentally, emotionally, physically, and socially. Thus, a pupil can become fascinated mentally when discussing a topic from a lesson or unit of study. When the teacher uses appropriate stress, pitch of words, enunciation, and juncture, pupils tend to listen and participate more fully. For example, if a teacher puts more stress on some words than others to make a points, this is quite different from teaching in a monotone voice. Stressing words differently in a sentence makes for enthusiasm for teaching by the teacher. Pitching words higher or lower as needed, also makes for lively instruction. If all words are pitched on the same level, a neutral effect occurs and pupils will feel the teacher is not enthused over what is being taught. Good enunciation emphasizes the importance of speaking clearly. Clarity in using one's voice may well make for improved communication with learners. Adults are well aware of individuals in society whose enunciation makes it difficult to understand what is intended. Increased difficulty is then involved in the communication arena.

Juncture, too, emphasizes the importance of communicating well among words in series with appropriate pauses, and at the end of a sentence depending if in written work a period, a question mark, or exclamation mark was used. Juncture should be related to punctuation marks used in written work. Video taping one's own teaching and observing the feedback may help the teacher to realize the importance of voice inflection with proper stress, pitch, enunciation and juncture.

Emotional involvement in learning emphasizes that the feelings of the learner are strongly involved with subject matter being learned. The pupil then might value highly what is taught. Beliefs are there which may well support the ideas as being worthy of acceptance. The teacher's emotions are such that he/she provides a model of that which is salient to learn. Valuing and prizing highly the educational enterprise is salient. The importance of learning is enhanced due to feelings involved in studying and achieving.

Physical involvement in learning pertains to a hands on approach as a means of achieving. Doing experiments and demonstrations, making things, and completing art projects may be used as means to show what has been learned in any curriculum area. There are a variety of ways to learn and indicate learnings acquired.

Socially, one can learn much. Through interaction with others, ideas are acquired assessed, and accepted, modified, or rejected. Social achievement also emphasizes being a part of a group. Belonging to a group and being wanted are goals of most and, perhaps, all learners. Being an isolate is indeed not a happy situation. Interaction with others provides a basis for learning, achieving, growing, and developing. Learning with others as well as by the self are two vital dimensions of acquiring knowledge, skills, and attitudes.

Interest in Learning

Interest in a lesson or unit of study needs to be developed within learners when it is lacking. If interest is already there, then it needs to be maintained. To develop interest, the teacher may assist pupils to secure background information for a new lesson or unit of study. The background information is presented inductively or deductively, but in a way to capture the inherent interests of those being taught. Interest in a topic is a powerful way of wanting to learn or having a desire to learn more on a selected topic. When pupils are interested, they usually move forward in achievement on their very own. The content studied and the pupil become one and not separate entities. Teachers, in many cases, can observe rather quickly if a pupil is or is not interested in what is being taught. It is a challenge to secure pupil interests so that learning becomes goal centred on the pupil's part.

Purpose in Learning

The teacher needs to guide pupils to perceive purpose in achieving vital objectives of instruction. Purpose emphasizes pupils accepting reasons for achieving specific objectives in the curriculum. Time taken to assist pupils to perceive purpose for learning is time well spent. The teacher may very briefly explain deductively why it is salient for the learner to learn selected knowledge or skills. Or, the teacher might raise a question as to why the new objective needs to be achieved and pupils may come up with possible answers. The latter approach is an inductive procedure in helping pupils perceive reasons for acquiring the new subject matter of skill. Adults can choose what they wish to learn and thus inwardly feel the need or purpose to do so. The pupil might have no choice in content and abilities to be learned and perceived purpose is then important to develop.

Meaning in Learning

Pupils as well as all individuals like to make sense out of what they are doing. If something does not make sense, it is meaningless to the intended person. Many times, pupils will memorize content for a test, but lack understanding of its meaning. Meaning theory is highly salient to emphasize. The teacher needs to be very careful in teaching so that learnings stressed to make sense to the pupil. If pupils respond in class with content that does not make sense, it is up to the teacher to clarify learnings in a caring manner. Teaching stresses clarification of ideas and making ideas so they are useful. Gestalt psychology stresses that an individual attempts to make something meaningful even thought it was not presented or perceived in that manner. Thus, what might be triangular, but is presented in line segments is perceived as a triangle. This may well be true if the line segments are completed with lines and vertexes making for a triangle. Or when a pupil is reading and does not know a word, he/she will fill in a word which to the reader makes sense. Expressions such as "meaningless work," "dead end jobs," or, "busy work" certainly does stress that which is meaningless and may be nonsense to the learner. Meaningful learnings are highly important for pupils in that new knowledge and skills to be acquired are built upon previous achievements. It behoove the teacher to assist pupils to extend that which has been learned. This can be done only of a solid foundation of meaning and making sense is in evidence.

Sequence in Learning

Pupils need to experience proper sequence in learning to achieve well. The order of ideas presented orally or in writing makes a lot of difference if a pupil is to comprehend subject matter. Thus, the teacher may jump forward in large leaps and pupils may not comprehend what is being presented. Or the content can become too repetitious, moving forward excessively slowly. Better it is if the pace of moving from the sampler to the more complex ideas is at a rate which the individual learner can comprehend. Most have listened to a speaker whose expressed ideas are sequenced so poorly that listeners lose out on what is being said. The jumps are too rapid in idea complexity or too slowly so as to make it appear as if duplicate content is being expressed. The teacher needs to pace ideas so that pupil understanding of subject matter is in evidence.

Programmed learning, be it in book form or computerised, has been developed and written by a programmer. It moves forward very slowly with the pupil reading a short selection of a few sentences. The pupil then responds to a multiple choice test item, covering content read. If he/she responds correctly, the pupil is rewarded. If the response was incorrect from the multiple choice test item, the learner now knows the correct answer from viewing the monitor and is also ready to read the next short reading of a few sentences before being tested in covering the content with a multiple choice test item. Read, respond, and check is used continuously in programmed learning. In most cases, the pupils responds correctly to a programme in programmed learning, if it has been field tested to take out the kinks. In good field tested programmes, the pupil may respond correctly 95% of the time. Why is the success rate that high? With a quality sequence or order of subject matter presented, the pupil experiences a high rate of success. One major problem, even thought the sequence is good, is the repetitious read, respond, and check approach in pupil's learning content. However, programmed learning has pointed out the importance of success and sequence in pupil learning.

PROVIDING FOR INDIVIDUAL DIFFERENCES

Pupils in a classroom differ from each other in a plethora of ways be it intellectually, in skill development, in motor coordination, in attitudinal achievement, and in aesthetic attainment. Somehow, the teacher must provide for all of these differences among learners in a classroom. It is indeed a complex task, but attempts must continually be made in that direction. Quality aide service should be available to each teacher under the latter's direction. The teacher should have major responsibility in determining the hiring and retention of teacher aides in the classroom. Since money for public schools tends to be scarce many times, there are good retired teachers who have stood the tests of morality, and of teaching skills and would be willing to volunteer a few hours each week to help pupils learn, in an agreed upon schedule. With early retirement of teachers in vogue, there are many who yearn to return to the classroom on a reduced, less strenuous situation, to volunteer their services. If paid teacher aids can be hired by a school, they should be provided inservice education to know what their duties and responsibilities would be.

Multiple Intelligences Theory emphasizes differences among children and how the child's strength may be used to show what has been learned and this would not stress the use of paper/pencil testing only. A variety of means would be used as indicated by the pupil's talents to show what has been achieved. Thus, a pupil might show in reading what has been achieved through an art project, a construction endeavour, one or more diagrams, and drawings, among others, to reveal comprehension of subject matter. Each pupil has needs which must be met in order that success in learning is to occur. Pupil progress needs to be monitored and assistance provided as needed (See Gardner, 1993).

Pupils individually also possess diverse styles of learning. These styles of learning need to be given ample consideration to the degree possible in a classroom. For example, selected pupils do learn better individually whereas others prefer to work together in cooperative learning. Perhaps, a balance between individual and group endeavours needs to be stressed for all pupils. This is true due to individuals in society doing things by the self as well as with others (See Searson and Dunn).

The Philosophy of Instruction

There are philosophical considerations which thoroughly impinge upon instructional decisions. Teachers need to know and understand different relevant philosophies and how they reflect instructional decision making. Each philosophy may be implemented in whole or in part. Generally, a teacher will follow an eclectic approach whereby several philosophies are used in planning and implementing the curriculum. Major philosophies need studying and analyzing, as well as implementing that which assists each pupil to learn as much as possible.

EXPERIMENTALISM AS A PHILOSOPHY OF EDUCATION

A teacher who reveals experimentalism as a philosophy of education has pupils engaging in problem solving activities. These pupils are not seated in rows and columns in the classroom, but rather work at different stations. The teacher guides pupils to identify a meaningful problem in context. The problem needs to be clear and capable of producing some kind of solution. An experimentalist cannot know the real world as it truly exists, but can experience nature and society only. Within experiences, individuals identify problems. Thus, within an ongoing unit of study, the pupil experiences and identifies a problem. The teacher serves to guide, challenge, and encourage pupil curiosity. With clarity involved in defining the problem, data needs gathering from a variety of reference sources to obtain necessary information related directly to the problem.

Data may come from a variety of reference sources. These include print materials such as textbooks, encyclopedias, basal textbooks, and library books as well as audio visual aids including illustrations, video tapes, films, filmstrips, slides, CD ROMS, and DVDs, among others. Objects and items need to be used, when relevant, in problem solving. Resource personnel and excursions could also appear under the heading of items and objects used in problem solving since an excursion, if taken, emphasizes reality. A resource person might bring in reality into his/her discussion with models, objects, and AV aids.

From relevant information gathered, the problem solver develops an hypothesis. The hypothesis is based on data which provided the needed information. Hypotheses are tentative and subject to revision. With doing more research, the tentative hypothesis is accepted, refused, or modified. New problems may well arise when data is gathered in answer to the hypothesis. Again, new problems identified need to possess clarity so that information from a variety of relevant sources may be secured. The information should relate directly to the identified problem. An hypothesis results which again is tentative and is subject to testing in a life like situation (See Ediger, 2001, 60-65).

To an experimentalist, truth is discovered through problem solving. One can never know ultimate reality and all hypotheses in problem solving are tentative and subject to change. For John Dewey, thinking becomes significant only when applied to life situations. It is, he has said, "an instrumentality used by man in adjusting himself to the practical situations in life." Or to phrase it more simply, human beings think in order to live. Because of this stimulus, which has its basis in biology and sociology, it is impossible—it is absurd—to interpret life in a systematic and abstract way. Since, moreover, Dewey held that life is in a constant flux, it is impossible to solve problems with any degree of finality for the problems of tomorrow will be different from those of today (Meyer, 1949).

Realism as a Philosophy of Education

Realists believe that one can know reality as it truly is, in whole or in part. To show this, one can observe diverse chemical formulas with its exact number of atoms which make up a compound or new substance. Thus H_2O and $C_6H_{12}O_6$ provide exact prescriptions in terms of what makes for a compound, such as water and sugar respectfully. No guess work is involved. Realists, too, like to be precise in what is observed and what is measured. They stress the science of education whereby objectives for pupil attainment are stated in measurable terms. With precise, measurably stated objectives, a pupil either does or does not attain them as a result of instruction. The objectives then provide direction to the teacher as to what is to be taught. The teacher does not need to guess which knowledge and skills are to be emphasised in teaching pupils. Presently, there are state mandated objectives, available to the teacher within their state, to use as benchmarks for instruction. The state mandated tests are aligned with these predetermined objectives. Both the objectives and the tests have been developed under the auspices of the involved state department of education. State mandated tests should be pilot tested on a specific set of pupils to take out kinks and weaknesses. In aligning the tests with the objectives within a state, validity of test items should be in the offing. The tests to be given pupils should then cover and be directly related to what has been taught in the classroom. If consistency of the same pupils' test results in the pilot study were in evidence, then reliability should be relatively high be it test/retest, split half, or alternative forms. Validity and reliability are two salient terms to stress in developing and implementing tests (See National Science Teachers Association, 2001).

With realism as a philosophy of education, exactness and precision become key words. Results from pupils' tests may be used to make comparisons among schools within a state. Reporting these comparisons in the media is known as a report card. Failing schools are identified. These are schools in which no or inadequate improvements occur in terms of test results from pupils. Two consecutive school years with inadequate test scores make for a designated failing school. Parents in these schools may then be able to use the school money spent by the district for their child, as vouchers, to attend to different school of their choice. The purpose of vouchers is to stress better teaching by emphasizing competition among schools which tend to harmonize with the free enterprise system of economics. Thus, parents may choose where to send their offspring to school to select the best education possible, just like individuals can shop for goods and services which are conceived to be the best available.

...One element that the various forms of realism do have in common is a rejection of the idealist's theory of knowledge that the various qualities of experience depend upon a knower for their experience. Realists believe that the universe is composed of real entities that exist in themselves. These entities can be known, and their existence is not dependent upon a knower or perceiver. Although realists can agree upon this point, they do not all agree when they attempt to build a metaphysical system. Here their views range from pluralism to dualism to monism. The realist's epistemological views include epistemological monism where it is held that objects are presented in consciousness, and epistemological dualism where objects are thought to be represented. The monists define mind as a relation between the organism and an object, while the dualists identify the mind more closely with the organisms. Realists do have a common tendency to view the world as the mechanism described by the physical sciences, and they generally believe in determinism, in orderliness in the universe. The unifying thesis of realism is that knowledge is thought to have a universal character and comes to man through his sensory capacity.... (Bowyer, 1970).

Idealism as a Philosophy of Education

Idealists believe in an idea centred world. They do not believe one can know ultimate reality as it truly is, but one can receive ideas pertaining to what is real. Ideas of reality can be known, but not the real things in and of themselves. Since obtained ideas are the important thing, it behooves the teacher to choose vital subject matter for pupil acquisition. Subject matter chosen for pupils to learn should contain relevant universals, concepts, and generalisations. An idealists curriculum can be quite abstract, but it must contain interest and challenge so that each pupil learns as much as possible. Selected idealists believe in metaphysics which emphasizes going beyond the reality which can be seen, felt, touched, tasted, and heard. In other words, reality here goes beyond the natural and social world to include the Absolute. The subjective manners, morals, and caring for others are very important to an idealist.

A teacher who is an idealist can stimulate much interest in the school curriculum by discussing with pupils fascinating open ended questions, covering content read by the learner. An open ended curriculum with fascinating questions may or may not stress problem solving. The child is being prepared for the future in idealism. The learnings acquired in school presently should guide the pupil to become a learned person in a democratic society. Vocational content is not too relevant for pupils but rather the basics in the curriculum need to stress that which is vital and salient. Higher levels of thinking are important when abstract ideas are emphasised in the curriculum. Thus, critical and creative thinking are very important for the pupil to become skilful in. Discussion of ideas gleaned from the different curriculum areas might well lead to higher levels of cognition.

The idealist says, in effect, if one seeks for elemental things, he will not find them in matter, motion, or force, but in reason, intelligence, personality, and values. Moreover, these realities have a cosmical significance; they are essences that bring order and unity into the universe. Hence, physical bodies and forces are secondary, being, as it were, externalisations or manifestations of the mind. Also, the ultimates do not depend upon human beings for their significance; they have independent existence (Wahlquist, 1942).

Mind is real and needs developing. What sets humans apart from the animal world is the mind and what it has to offer. Mental achievements are of greatest value. A quality liberal arts curriculum can provide the individual with the necessary ingredients to develop well intellectually. The objectives in general education needs to be challenging mentally. The mind needs to be stimulated with learning opportunities which motivate to reach higher levels of objectives. The person must will to achieve, grow, and develop.

The heart of idealism is the belief that basic reality consists of ideas, thoughts, minds or substantive selves, not to physical matter. Since priority is given to minds, minds have bodies, but bodies do not have minds. Idealism usually carries with its views the idea of the subsistence (the superexistence) of God, who also is basically mind or self. The universe is an expression of intelligence and will; its order is due to an eternal, spiritual reality. For idealists, people are good—active substantive minds; they are absolutely real selves endowed with free will or genuine moral choice (Bigge, 1982).

Existentialism as a Philosophy of Education

Existentialists believe that each person is and comes into the world without any purposes. Thus, the individual must seek and find purpose or reasons for living. These purposes are not given to a person who did not ask to be born There is complete freedom for each person to become the kind of individual desired. Choices among alternatives need to be made continually, if the desire is there to do so or not. Dread might well be there in making these decisions. Choices may make for alienation. To an existentialist, life is absurd and ridiculous. Knowledge is subjective to the person, never objective. To be a human being, one needs to make authentic choices; no one should make decisions for another individual. An open ended curriculum needs to exist so that the learner may continually practice decision making. Choices may be made in terms of objectives to achieve, learning opportunities to pursue, or assessment procedures to use in ascertaining how much has been learned.

Man is nothing else but what he makes of himself. Such is the first principle of existentialism. It is also what is called subjectivity, the name we are labelled with when charges are brought against us. But what we do mean by this, if not that man has a greater dignity than a stone or a table? For we mean that man first exists, that is, that man first of all is the being who hurls toward a future and who is conscious of imagining himself as being in the future. Man is at the start of a plan which is aware of the self.... (Alston and Brandt, 1978).

Teachers and administrators need to study, analyze, and implement selected tenets of philosophical thought as each might assist pupils to achieve more optimally. Schools of thought in the philosophy of education might well help to improve the curriculum as well as provide for individual differences.

REFERENCES

1. Alston, William P., and Richard B. Brandt (1978), *The Problems of Philosophy.* The Edition. Boston: Allyn and Bacon, Inc., 257-258.
2. Bowyer, Carlton H. (1970), *Philosophical Perspectives for Education.* Glenview, Illinois: Scott, Foresman and Company, 17.
3. Bigge, Morris (1982), *Education Philosophies for Teachers.* Columbus, Ohio: Charles E. Merrill Publishing Company, 25.

4. Ediger, Marlow (2001), *"Mathematics as Communication,"* School Science, 34(4), 60-65.
5. Ediger, Marlow, and Digumarti Bhaskara Rao (2003). *Philosophy and Curriculum.* New Delhi: Discovery Publishing House, India.
6. Gardner, Howard (1993), *Multiple Intelligences:* Theory Into Practice, New York: Basic Books.
7. Meyer, Adolph E. (1949), *The Development of Education in the Twentieth Century.* Englewood Cliffs, New Jersey: Prentice-Hall, Inc., 42-43.
8. National Science Teachers Association (2001), Classroom Assessment and the National Education Standards. Washington, DC: the Association, NSTA.
9. Searson, Robert, and Rita Dunn (2001), *"The Learning Styles Teaching Model,"* Science and Children, 38(5), 22-36.
10. Wahlquist, John T. (1942), *The Philosophy of American Education.* New York: Ronald Press Company, 46, 47.

Important Historical Events in the Curriculum

A plethora of events can be listed which assisted in the historical development of the curriculum. The salient from the lesser important needs to be chosen when listing what is important in the history of teaching and learning. It might be too, that an individual credited with doing something vitally significant in the past had others who also practiced the same thing, sequentially or simultaneously. The author will list and discuss selected important happenings in the curriculum. From that time on, additional changes occurred in the instructional arena.

John Locke and the Curriculum

John Locke (1632-1704) was an early advocate that school should be a pleasant place to learn. In his day, teaching pupils in school resulted in endless beatings, whippings, and sarcasm. School then was a very unpleasant place to be. Rather, Locke advocated that learning should be interesting to pupils. He believed in the Tabula Rosa theory whereby a pupil had a mind like a blank sheet with nothing printed thereon initially. With good teaching, as a model, the mind imprints positive things. The teacher then is a model for pupils to emulate pertaining to what is taught.

Instead of rote learning and drill which was prevalent for pupils in his day, Locke emphasised that pupils learned through the five senses and then the mind operated upon these items. The mind then reflected upon sense input to come up with reflections such as doubting, willing, accepting, modifying, rejecting and relating. Lock's contributions emphasised thinking about what had been taken in by the senses. School was more than drill and memorisation. Then too, Locke stressed four broad objectives of education in sequential importance:

1. Goal # one: virtue which stressed living a decent life and refraining from evil.
2. Goal # two: wisdom whereby a person develops foresight in order to make appropriate choices in life.
3. Goal # three: good breeding which stresses being able to work well with others and having good manners.
4. Goal # four: knowledge objectives which needed to be achieved. Salient, vital ends in subject matter then become important in the number four position (See Brubacher, 1966).

These four broad objectives emphasize that knowledge alone is not adequate for a pupil to achieve, but being a well adjusted person is equally salient. Goals one through three present objectives which are very worthwhile for pupils to achieve but do not appear in present state mandated tests due to their lack of measurability. Even though John Locke made his proposals in the seventeenth century, his goals on reflection pertaining to what was learned through the senses (sensation) are also minimal or many state mandated tests. Certainly, Locke's concepts of doubting, modifying, rejecting, and relating, of ideas are equality important presently when reading content. He believed that education is more of a process than a product. Ulich (1950) wrote the following pertaining to Locke's emphasis upon attitudinal development within students:

> Starting from the conception that knowledge has to foster, rather than to impede, the growth of an all rounded personality, Locke demanded a method of education apt to encourage initiative, independent judgment, observation, and critical use of reason. He wanted languages taught by conversation, not by grammatical exercises and memorisation; generally speaking, he preferred learning by doing to learning by imitation...

Many of John Locke's ideas on education are still important today.

Johann Friedrich Pestalozzi and the Curriculum

Johann Friedrich Pestalozzi (1746-1827) advocated the use of the object lesson in teaching. The lesson then would stress the use of real objects in teaching. Thus, if pupils were to read about a "dog," a model of this animal or an actual dog would be shown to children. Children then associate the word "dog" with the actual or model dog. Reality was always related to the abstract. In Pestalozzi's day, the abstract and rote learning alone were emphasised and pupils would be drilled until mastery occurred. Corporal punishment was used if pupils did not achieve what the teacher wanted them to learn. Pestalozzi stressed that schooling should be a joyous place to be and humane methods of instruction should be used. Learning should be natural, not coercive. Rivalry and fear should not be used to motivate pupils to learn since each pupil is different in talents and abilities. There should be no gulf between home and school; both should work together for the good of the child. Each pupil has inherent powers to use in learning. Good will should respect these abilities and talents. Pestalozzi was altruistic; he saw the gulf between the rich and the poor and wished their elimination. The children from wealthier homes looked down upon those from poorer home situations. Pestalozzi believed in raising humanity to new heights. The individual must be developed to new heights with his/her personal progress. Each person must have dignity and worth. Society must provide opportunities for the ethical and social growth of each pupil. All facets of a pupil need to be developed—the intellectual, the moral, and the physical side. Human beings are a unity and cannot be divided into component parts.

In sequence, learning should move from the simple to the complex as well as from the concrete to the abstract. The teacher is like a gardner; he/she helps pupils to unfold in terms of growth in the natural environment (Eby, 1964).

From the thinking of Pestolozzi, the following are considered highly important for present day teachers:

1. his emphasis upon using concrete materials of instruction with object lessons.
2. his emphasis upon quality pupil sequence, such as teachers moving from the simple to the complex.
3. his emphasis upon the school being a pleasant place for learning including an appropriate environment.
4. his emphasis upon high respect for pupils and children.
5. his emphasis upon development of the total pupil such as intellectual, moral, physical, and emotional.

Johann Friedrich Herbart and Sequence in Learning

Johann Friedrich Herbart (1776-1841) had his own teacher training school whereby he practiced his theories of education. There were five steps of teaching which Herbart believed to be essential. The first step emphasised that teachers prepared learners for the ensuing lesson. This was the step of preparation. Thus, a pupil needed background information to benefit from the new lesson. This step sounds familiar to teachers today when they assist pupils to obtain needed background information to benefit from the selection to be read. Step two, the teacher presented the new lesson directly related to the step of preparation. Pupils were to perceive the relationship and not be left with isolated thoughts. The learner then associated the new with the old learnings in step three, which is association. This assisted pupils to develop one or more generalisations. The generalisation(s) guided pupils to further relate ideas in reading. Step five emphasised "use." Pupils were to use that which had been learned so that better retention, rather than forgetting would occur.

As we already know, good instruction uses the incentive inherent in interest. For this purpose, the teacher must find out what kind of presentation and learning is commensurate with the child's capacity. Otherwise the school obstructs rather than assists the growth of the child's personality. On the other hand, every individual lives in society and must learn to comply with objective standards and characteristics of every civilisation. The more advanced such a civilisation is, the less can be individual be permitted simply to follow his likes and affections; rather, he must be able to direct them so that his individuality surves the civilisation in and on which it thrives. Only, in such ways can an individual be productive and feel himself free and happy.

Hence, there arises for the teacher, on the one hand, the obligation to cultivate the interests of the child, in order to stimulate the spontaneity; on the other hand the need not only to cultivate the child's personal interests, but to introduce him to variety of human knowledge and experiences in order to help him in the appreciation of he fundamental values of civilised societies. Such an education, Herbart would call a "liberal education."

Herbart believed strongly in character education. A study of literature and history were the two best academic areas to stress character development. Here, pupils may emulate those traits and characteristics which make for good character. Herbart identified the following standards making for curriculum improvement:

1. building background information within pupils before pursuing the new lesson.
2. stimulate interest in reading.
3. relate ideas read, the past with the present.
4. guide pupils to generalize on ideas read, not accept ideas in isolation only.
5. help pupils to apply what was learned and achieved.

Pertaining to Herbart, Bowyer (1970) wrote:

One of the most important and lasting contributions that Herbart made to pedagogical theory is the doctrine of interest. Interest, according to Herbart, is some inner tendency, an active power residing in the mind that urges the retention of a concept (an object of thought) in the conscientiousness or a return to the object of consciousness. The tendency is increased by the law of frequency and by the law of association. The primary task of the educator is to present the ideas constantly and consistently to the attention of the child. In this way the teacher is able to control the experiences of the child, and to provide him with the sorts of insight that will mature his judgment.

A recognition of the moral law is acted out by an exhibition of good judgment, decisiveness, warmth, and self restraint. In all regards, and children should be educated to will the good so freely and consistently that it becomes second nature. Since it is impossible to foresee what the choices and goals of the man will be, it depends upon the teacher to prepare the child with principles that should guide the normal man to good choices and with abilities and qualifications that will enable the man to attain his goals. Therefore, it is highly essential for the instruction to cover a wide range of subjects.

Herbart believed that individuals were born as neutral beings, not good nor as sinful, bad persons. Sin being a part of the individual's lot at birth was dismissed by Herbart. People could become evil growing up in a negative environment. Each person then learns from the surrounding environment. Whatever society is like imprints itself upon the human mind, according to Herbart.

Friedrich William Froebel and the Curriculum

Friedrich William Froebel (1782-1852) is credited with bringing the kindergarten movement into being. He believed strongly in pupils being creative beings. This idea was far removed from the teaching practices of his day whereby pupils were to be conformists to adult demands, such as being seen but not heard, and learning by memorisation of subject matter. To be creative in kindergarten, Froebel emphasised the use of three kinds of learning activities for pupils:

- gifts had to do with pupils manipulating geometric figures such as cubes, lines, points, rectangular solids, cylinders, spheres, and pyramids, among others. When using these geometrical models, pupil creativity was revealed through the making of different structures. These structures included the building of houses, barns, castles, and cottages, among others. Originality in developing these structures and uses made of gifts fascinated Froebel. These uses could include building a larger cube from the smaller ones and then reduce the larger cube to the smaller original cubes. Smaller cylinders could be placed inside the larger cylinder. In return, the larger cylinder could be taken apart and separate cylinders would result.

- occupations stressed the importance of materials used such as clay to make an animal, for example. Occupations emphasised the use of a material such as clay to make something else. Paper cutting also indicated how a material could be altered. Thus, a sheet of paper could be folded several times and a bird cut from the folded paper resulting in several birds from the newly unfolded paper. Use of water colours, pencil sketching, and coloured dots placed on a sheet to make a design, were further examples of occupations. With occupations, the form and shape of the original materials had been altered.
- mother play songs stressed the importance of children creatively dramatizing what was sung. For example, if pupils sang a song pertaining to raising garden crops, each would dramatize what was sung. A child hen while singing might dramatize planting seeds, hoeing weeds, watering the plants, and harvesting the crops. The child involved would dramatize what was sung.

Friedrich Froebel had tremendous influence in changing the curriculum such as in:

- pupils being encouraged to develop unique ideas in the school curriculum rather than duplicating what others had completed. Novel, unique ideas were wanted.
- pupils were to be taught by trained teachers using Froebel's methodology.
- pupils had definite materials of instruction to use in the classroom and school environment whereby

the end result would be a creative product, involving a unique process.

- pupils were to be highly accepted by others in the school and community environment.
- pupils were encouraged to exhibit creative behaviour, not pattern their products pertaining to what others had done. They were born with creative tendencies according to Froebel (Ediger, 1988, 3).

Creative behaviour is prised highly prised in today's classroom. Clay modelling, for example, is just as important presently in kindergarten as compared to Froebel's day.

Friedrich William Froebel believed that pupils at birth were born as good, not depraved individuals. The goodness needs to be brought out from within the individual with creative behaviour. In Froebel's day, the thinking was that pupils were born as evil, sinful beings. These pupils then brought forth bad behaviour which was within the child. Using gifts, occupations, and mother play songs, the goodness of each individual is brought forth with creativity as an end goal (Ediger and Rao, 2003, Chapter One).

Kierkegaard and the Curriculum

Soren Kierkegaard (1813-1855) emphasised life as being subjective and filled with the many choices to be made. A philosophy of existentialism was then born. Each decision to be made, from among alternatives, emphasizes subjectivity, not objectivity. Kierkegaard stressed the importance of pupils making choices and decisions. This is what life is about. One first exists and then finds his/her essence of purposes in life. These are not given, but must be sought and found. It is up to the individual to find his/her own essences or purposes in life. Each individual chooses and cannot blame others for the consequences of personal choices made. There must be complete freedom to make these choices. Kierkegaard emphasised existentialism as a philosophy of life. Existentialists believe in the following concepts which are faced by human beings in life's daily situations: feelings of dread, alienation, loneliness, guilt, fear of death, as well as happiness.

Kierkegaard emphasised that there are three stages of development which individuals go through in terms of morality. These are:

1. stage one ... the aesthetic phase. Here, the individual decides for the self what to do with little concern for others. The self alone is what is important in life. It definitely is a selfish stage of living. Everything centres around the self.
2. stage two ... the ethical phase. Here, the individual is interested in making authentic decisions. Commitments are made. Strong feelings of anxiety, and tension are in evidence. Choices are made which are awe inspiring, dreaded in the making, and might well make for alienation. Being aware of death and one's final days make for better deeds and acts by the involved person. To live a quality life, one must live as if this day is the last. One needs to know the self well in order to make quality, authentic choices which are a duty to fulfil.
3. stage three. Here, a leap of faith needs to be made in moving from stage two to stage three, which stresses humanness and a desire for the good. Being an authentic being, not a facade, is important in baring oneself to others as one truly is. Being conscientious and having a strong will is needed to possess the ideals of stage three. Faith overcomes doubt and despair (See Galbraith and Jones for discussion in comparing Piaget's and Kohlberg's theories of moral development, 1975).

When making choices from among alternatives, subjectivity is involved. Decisions cannot be made objectively since the human being weighs the values of each choice and then makes a decision as to which one to pursue. There is uncertainty when choices are made in life's arena. There can even be fear and trembling, a human condition in being a moral person in society in relating to others (Ediger and Rao, 2003, Chapter Eight).

It has been a long standing goal, since the early 1900s, for pupils to be able to choose and make decisions. Being able to make good choices/decisions is perhaps as admirable goal as possible to emphasize in the curriculum as well as in life. Each person is bombarded with opportunities and chances to choose. Will the involved person then make good choices?

Learning centres in the classroom provide opportunities for each pupil to select sequential learning activities. If there are seven learning centres in the classroom with four learning activities listed on each task card per centre, there are a total of 28 tasks from which pupils might choose sequentially to participate in. The teacher introduces the centres briefly to pupils and then learners individually may select the centre and sequential tasks to work on. Perseverance is needed to complete each sequential task chosen. There needs to be a commitment to complete what is chosen and be punctual in producing quality work. There is much freedom for the pupil to make choices in terms of learning activities to pursue. The pupil needs to be responsible to do quality work. There is an advantage in pupils working at learning centres in each academic area:

1. the pupil gets to complete what is desired and self selected, rather than someone else doing the choosing of what might not have perceived purpose of value.
2. the pupil may work at his/her optimal speed in completing a learning activity rather than

someone else making unrealistic time demands in completing an activity.

3. the pupil may select what he/she can benefit most from developmentally, rather than an imposed learning activity which might be too complex or too easy and lacks challenge (See Eisner, 2002).

An individualised reading programme might well tress library book titles which deal with the feelings of individuals as indicated by existentialists. A wide variety of titles and genres need to be in the offing for the child to make authentic choices as to what to read. The benefits of individualised reading to pupils are the following:

1. the pupil may select library books sequentially which capture personal interests.
2. the pupil may choose library books to read which are on his/her own unique reading level.
3. the pupil may pace his/her own optimal reading level.
4. the pupil who likes to learn by the self, as a learning style, has opportunities to do so.
5. the pupil may have a conference with the teacher after the completion of reading a library book. Here, the learner may reveal his achievement in the completed library book and indicate feelings he/she has toward the content read (Ediger, 2002, 107-110).

In individualised reading, the learner is in control of what is to be read. Decision making is important in individualised reading.

In the original version of individualised reading, teachers held individual conferences with students. In a reading workshop, teachers hold group as well as individual conferences. At the heart of the workshop is the time when student read self selected books, respond to their reading, or engage in group or individual conferences. Self selected reading may last approximately thirty minutes or longer. If available, the time may be extended. Because students will be reading their self selected books independently they should be encouraged to use appropriate strategies. Before reading, they should survey, predict, and set a purpose for reading. As they read, they should use summarizing, inferencing, and imaging strategies—if appropriate—and should monitor for meaning. As they read, students can use sticky notes to indicate a difficult word or puzzling passage...

Response time may last thirty minutes or longer. During response time, students may meet in a literature discussion groups to discuss their reading, write in their journals, work on an extension activity, plan a reader's theater or other type of presentation, work at one of the classroom's centres, continue to read, or attend a conference. During response time, hold individual or group conferences. If time allows, circulate around the room, giving help and guidance as needed. Visiting literature circles should be a priority (Gunning, 2000).

Charles Sanders Pierce and Experimentalism

Charles Sanders Pierce (1839-1914) was an early advocate of pupils engaging in problem solving activities. The consequences of an act are the most salient in problem solving. Ideas can be tested in action to see which work and which are of little value. Thus, if two ideas are tested in a life like situation, the consequences of each are noticed. Ideas have to be relevant and vital to be tested. If the consequences of each idea do not matter when tested, they have no worth. One looks at the results, not the intent, to notice the cash value of each idea. This is opposite of learning something for its own sake, since Pierce's philosophy of experimentalism advocated looking at results/

consequences to see what has value and what works (Ediger, 1995, 63-64).

Pierce looked upon belief as occupying the very important middle position between thought and action. Beliefs guide our desires and shape our actions. But beliefs are "unfixed" by doubts. It is when the "irrigation of doubt" causes a struggle to attain belief that the enterprise of thought begins. Through doubt, we try to fix our beliefs so that we have a guide for action. There are several ways in which we can fix our beliefs, according to Pierce. There is the method of tenacity, whereby people cling to their beliefs, refusing to entertain doubts about them or consider arguments or evidence for another view. Another method is to invoke authority, as when persons in authority require the acceptance of certain ideas as true on pain of punishment. Still another method is that the metaphysician or philosopher such as Plato, Descartes, or Hegel, according to Pierce, would settle questions of belief by asking whether an idea was "agreeable to reason." With all these methods Pierce found himself in agreement precisely because they could not, in his view, achieve their intent, namely to fix or settle belief. What they all lacked was some connection with experience and behaviour.

Pierce therefore offered a fourth, the method of science, whose chief virtue, he thought, was its realistic basis in experience. Unlike the methods of tenacity, authority, and reason, all of which rest upon what a person possesses within his own mind as a consequence solely of his thinking, the method of science is built on the assumption that there are real things, the characteristics of which are entirely independent of our opinions about them. Moreover because these real things affect our senses according to regular laws, we can assume they will affect each observer the same way. Beliefs that are grounded in such real things can be verified, and their "fixation" can be a public act rather than a private one. There is in fact no way to agree or disagree with a conclusion arrived at by means of the first three methods since they refer to nothing whose consequence or real existence can be tested... (Stumpf, 1971, 405-406).

Problem solving is important presently and, no doubt, will always remain salient. Each person has problems and needs to identify them, whether in the school curriculum or in society. Each problem needs clear identification. Information needs to be obtained to solve the problem. The information, acquired from a variety of sources, needs to be tested in life like situations. That which works as a solution presents a desired course of action.

REFERENCES

1. Bowyer, Carlton (1970), *Philosophical Perspectives for Education.* Glenview, Illinois: Scott, Foresman and Company, 252-253.
2. Brubacher, John (1966), *A History of the Problems of Education.* New York: McGraw Hill, Inc.
3. Eby, Frederick (1964), *The Development of Modern Education.* Second Edition. Englewood Cliffs, New Jersey: Prentice—Hall, Inc. 431-469.
4. Ediger, Marlow (1995), *Philosophy in Curriculum Development,* Kirksville, Missouri: Simpson Publishing Company, 63-74.
5. Ediger, Marlow (1988), *Language Arts Curriculum in the Elementary School.* Kirksville, Missouri: Simpson Publishing Company, p. 3.
6. Ediger, Marlow (2002), *"Pedagogical Considerations in Reading."* Experiments in Education, 30(6), 107-110.
7. Ediger, Marlow, and D. Bhaskara Rao (2003), *Language Arts Curriculum.* New Delhi, India: Discovery Publishing Company, Chapter One.
8. Ediger, Marlow, and D. Bhaskara Rao (2003), *Philosophy and Curriculum.* New Delhi, India: Discovery Publishing House, Chapter Eight.
9. Eisner, Elliot (2002), *"The Kind of School We Need."* Phi Delta Kappan, 83(8), 576-594.

10. Galbraith, Ronald E., and Thomas M. Jones (1975), *"Teaching Strategies for Moral Dilemmas: An Application of Kohlberg's Theory of Moral Development in the Classroom."* Social Education, 39(1), 16-22.

11. Gunning, Thomas (2000), *Creating Literacy Instruction for all Children.* Needham Heights, MA: Allyn and Bacon, p. 400.

12. Stumpf, Samuel Enoch 91971), *Philosophy, History and Problems.* New York: Mc Graw Hill Book Company, 406-407.

13. Ulich, Robert, *History of Educational Thought.* New York: American Book Company, 208.

Psychology of Parental Involvement in the Curriculum

Parent/teacher conferences are a must to secure parental cooperation in the education of their offspring. The support and inclusion of parents can make for an improved curriculum for pupils. There is much that parents can tell the teacher about their child in the school setting. Also, parents can benefit much from the teacher of their children in a quality conference. There needs to be mutual acceptance and respect for both the parents and the teacher. Nothing is basically accomplished in a hostile environment. Careful listening is a necessity during the conference. The teacher needs to feel that parents can offer much information which can be used in teaching and learning situations for an improved curriculum (See also, Chall, 1983).

Parental Input Into a Conference

What can parents contribute to the parent/teacher conference? They can discuss interests that the pupil has and may bring these into the curriculum. A hobby possessed by the child can be brought into sharing time as an opening exercise item. During sharing time, the child may gain feelings of belonging by telling about his/her hobby. Esteem and recognition needs might also be met. Pupils tend to like to share hobbies with others in the classroom. Questions may be raised by pupils pertaining to the hobby. If possible, the hobby should be shown to pupils. Actually showing the hobby represents a concrete experience. Meaning can then be attached much sooner to a hobby as compared to telling about it only or largely. The degree of interest which pupils show in the hobby by the presenter needs to be observed by the teacher. The teacher might be able to assist the sharer in locating more information related to the hobby. An increased amount of reading may then accrue. The involved learner may do selected writing experiences directly related to the hobby, such as writing a poem or story. When reading the written product to peers, the child might well experience oral communication skills. When listening to others tell about their individual hobbies, the child's listening skills are reinforced or improved upon.

Second, the teacher might learn what children like in school as learning opportunities. The feeling dimension is involved here. Thus, a parent may say that a child prefers to work by the self rather than with others. A style of learning is then emphasised. The teacher might then wish to arrange learning opportunities whereby the child can excel on an individual basis. Committee learnings are salient, also, since people do associate with others in society as well as work by the self.

Third, parents may praise the teacher for selected improvements made in a child's learning. Teachers are human and do like to have their contributions rewarded and encouraged. Perhaps, the teacher may wish to extend those learnings more frequently in classroom teaching. Whatever is rewarded and encouraged should then be examined by the teacher and more of those things implemented in classroom teaching.

Fourth, parents might offer ideas on what they deem as important from the child's point of view, such as sustained silent reading (SSR) in the classroom. Pupils choosing what is of interest to them in reading may well have much benefit to the child. A child centred curriculum has recommend benefits.

Fifth, the parent may suggest what the child needs more help in, such as in developing selected word recognition skills. The parent might have noticed in the home setting how the child cannot associate certain sounds with their related individual letters or graphemes. When consistent, it is vital that pupils develop skill in associating graphemes and their individual sound. Phonics might well help these pupils to become more proficient readers.

Sixth, parent/teacher conferences offer opportunities to get to know each other as human beings as well as develop rapport, Good rapport is needed in order for the educational process to move forward. Mistrust is a negative concept when conducting parent/teacher conferences.

Thus, parents may help the teacher in assisting their offspring to achieve more optimally, including feelings of concern for a possession of social development skills. Interacting well is vital in getting along with others in school and in society (Ediger, 1994, 29-31).

Parent/Teacher Conferences

Parent/teacher conferences should be held at least two times a year. This makes it possible to compare the first with the second conference for each child. The chairs for the conference should be comfortable and make for a face to face situation in communication. The teacher needs to be well prepared for each conference. Pupil products from school work should be available for viewing. Thus the teacher may show what a child has completed in reading such as written work, drawings to reveal reading comprehension, diagrams and maps to show the setting of a story read, cassette recordings of pupil oral reading, work book pages of purposeful activities, pupil self evaluation sheet, teacher appraisal of pupil achievement in reading based on quality criteria, among others. This provides opportunities to share pupil achievement with parents. Selected pupils have portfolios for parents to view. These portfolios contain a variety of kinds of materials to show learner achievement in schoolwork. The following may be chosen by the pupil with teacher guidance for placement in a reading portfolio:

1. outlines, summaries, written book reports, critiques, letters to the editor, and journal entries.
2. cassette recordings of oral book reports, discussions within committee, and oral reading.
3. snapshots of projects developed to show comprehension of content such as murals, construction work, art endeavours, pencil sketching, creative and formal dramatics, and diagrams.
4. self assessment in terms of quality criteria.
5. test scores on teacher written tests. (Ediger, 1997, 1-6).

Items and entries in the portfolio may be shown and discussed with parents. The involved pupil may tell of his/her portfolio to parents. Possible questions and comments on the portfolio may be discussed with parents.

With state mandated objectives and tests, there are certainly a plethora of questions which parents might well raise. These questions might involve the following:

1. what if a pupil fails the test on a specific grade level, will he/she be promoted to the next grade? The revised ESEA Act requires children in grades

three through eight and grade ten to be tested. One possibility is that the child may be held back and repeat the grade in which failure resulted in test taking. Selected states have easier tests and higher passing rates than do others.

2. will failing a test make for more pupils dropping out before the high school years end? What do dropouts do who have no high school diploma in a competitive environment?

3. how often might a pupil fail a state mandated test and still be able to take it over?

4. can a pupil possess degrees of certainty that what is on the stated mandated test has been covered by objectives achieved in class? Validity of a test is always important to the test taker. The author remembers taking standardised tests which he deemed had items not covered in class. In supervising university student teachers, he heard many pupils say after taking a test, "but we did not have that in class!" It is also possible for a person to forget what actually was taught in the classroom.

5. how can I assist my child to be ready for the oncoming state mandated test?

6. are there additional considerations for a pupil passing on to the next grade level other than a single test score?

7. can machine scored tests be incorrectly tabulated due to glitches?

8. what kind of a curriculum will be experienced by a pupil who fails a state mandated test and is not promoted to the next grade level?

9. why does a single test score determine an individual's future?

10. should additional means be used to ascertain a child's achievement, other than a test score? (Ediger, 2001, ERIC, ED455498).

The above named questions are highly valid to discuss with the teacher and, if possible, with the school principal. Parents have concerns about their child's future. Certainly, parents should have the best information possible for decision making pertaining to their offspring. During parent/teacher conference as well as all questions which parents have should be answered honestly and courteously. If the information is not available at the time parents ask, retrieval of needed content should be a primary goal and it should be provided to the parent. Pupils and parents' feelings need to be respected. It is good to praise efforts of parents put forth in educating their children in the home setting. Parents, too, having needs for recognition. The teacher should have available selected ways in which parents can assist the teacher in helping learners achieve in school such as reading stories aloud to their children. There needs to be developed within parents feelings of belong to school and to the community (Ediger, 2001, ERIC, 456412).

Developing a Learning Community

How can a community spirit be developed within parents, teachers, principals, and the lay public? Togetherness feelings then need to be in the offing. There are shared goals which need to be achieved within the community so all might benefit from the good life. It is good to have shared decision making when developing a community of learners. Encouragement needs to be there for all in a community to participate in developing a community of learners. Leadership responsibilities and positions should be cooperatively developed. Chairpersons chosen should have a caring, helping philosophy. Frequent rotation of leaders is salient. Each person, to the best possible, should have opportunities to serve as a leader. Encouragement here is a necessity. Ideas for an agenda should come from stakeholders in the community. Careful listening to the thinking of others is paramount. Active involvement is salient on the part of all involved in developing a community of learners. This includes listening, speaking, reading, and writing, the four skills needed by all to communicate well with others and establish a model in their use in school and in society. Conducting a meeting requires the cooperation of all involved in the community of participants. Each needs to learn and implement the concept of group dynamics in order to have a model for individual and group participation in the educational enterprise. Improving the curriculum is the purpose of a community of learners. Not only should the school curriculum be improved but also the educational experiences of all in the community of learners. Feelings of belonging for all is a necessity. Developing feelings of belonging as well as having status are important to all in the community of learners. Participants need to learn as much as possible about the school curriculum and how it affects pupils in the school setting. Much learning accrues when community members interact with each other (Ediger, 2001, ERIC, ED 456411).

Community members need to develop feelings of respect and acceptance in order to identify and solve curricular problems. Data needs to be gathered individually and collectively in order to solve problems. A tentative hypothesis should result in answer to the problem(s). Each hypothesis needs to be evaluated in a life like situation. Hypotheses need to be changed as evidence warrants. Hypotheses to improve the curriculum should be tried out in a school setting. The local classroom setting needs continual appraisal as well as improvements made. Feedback from the tryouts should be evaluated and revisions made to the original teaching plans, if necessary.

Other teachers should be encouraged to study and, if acceptable, try out the new teaching suggestions in the classroom. A newsletter should be sent to all participants in the learning community. The news media might also be used to communicate efficiently with others. Communication skills need to be developed and refined within the group of participants.

Relevant problems for participants to work on include the following:

1. how to choose library books for home reading?
2. how to read aloud to young children at home so they become enthused readers?
3. how to assist pupils in the home setting to recognize unknown words?
4. how to guide pupils to understand and attach meaning to what is being read?
5. how to encourage pupil reading activities in the home setting as well as at school?
6. how to assist pupils to reflect upon what has been read?
7. how to motivate pupils in desiring to do more reading?
8. how to provide a learning environment in the home setting to facilitate pupil reading?
9. how to involve older siblings in helping young learners in reading achievement?
10. how to assist pupils in test taking when state mandated tests are forthcoming. Tests cause much anxiety on the part of pupils and parents, especially when high stakes are involved? (Ediger, 2001, ERIC, ED452486).

Problem areas become important to identity and achieve closure in order for pupils to benefit from the community of learners. Parents as partners is a major goal to attain in working toward better pupil achievement. Committees may be arranged in which parents in small groups study and deliberate vital solutions to those important problem areas being pursued. Consultant help may be provided as needed. The community of learners should try out new ideas, with their offspring, in the home setting and report back to the entire group pertaining to the obtained results (See also, Buettner, 2002).

Viewing Pupil Results

The community of learners needs to view evidence of pupil achievement. The pupil's identity needs to be kept anonymous when observing written work and other products of learner achievement. Video tapes, purchased commercially, may be played of actual classroom settings to analyze strengths and weaknesses in teaching pupils. These might be ordered from a commercial company. Common problems of pupil achievement may be diagnosed and remedies suggested. It is good for the community of learners to keep a set of recommended psychological guidelines in mind when evaluating and implementing teaching improvement. The following guidelines are salient:

1. pupils need to be guided to stay on task.
2. pupil interests need consideration when choosing learning opportunities.
3. pupils need to experience intrinsic reasons for achieving.
4. pupils need to be actively involved in the ongoing learning activity.
5. pupils need to develop and maintain attitudes of accepting others as human beings having much worth.

6. pupils need to get along well with others.
7. pupils need to do reflective thinking on what has been achieved and what is left to achieve.
8. pupils need to achieve continuous progress in the curriculum. Feelings of inadequacy and doubt will accrue without planning for it.
9. pupils need to develop feelings of security in the classroom, with teacher assistance, to attain affective objectives pertaining to belongingness in the classroom.
10. pupil curriculum development involving the community of learners with careful planning and deliberation of ideas for each meeting (See Searson and Dunn).

There are school sponsorship of events in which the community of learners should receive considerable positive learnings. Open house is held in most schools toward the beginning of the new school year. Here, parents have an opportunity to meet the teachers of their children. There are chances to discuss briefly any problem faced by the child in school. These may be academic, social, and/or emotional. The point being that here are opportunities to begin necessary communication with the teacher about the involved child's progress in school.

There are diverse media which may be used to communicate with parents whereby the face to face parent/ teacher might well be supplemented with more convenient ways of communication. The telephone is a useful method. Messages may be communicated via telephone even though the parent is not home. Thus, the voice recorder may communicate a message such as complementing how well the offspring did on a project. Parents do like to hear from the teacher frequently to notice positive messages about the child's progress. E-mail messages sent to parents can be quite effective in communicating how well, specifically, the child is doing in school. Fax is another quality instantaneous way of communicating ideas to parents. Snail mail, or letter writing and sending, are still effective ways of communication. Which messages may be communicated in a non-face to face approach?

1. improvement in a child's oral reading.
2. good behaviour shown in the school cafeteria.
3. working together well with others on a group project.
4. doing well in sustained silent readying (SSR).
5. being attentive in class discussions.
6. achievement in written work.
7. completing class work on time.
8. assisting others to achieve in class, as needed.
9. peer teaching within a small group which needs assistance.
10. the child pronouncing words, as necessary, to others during silent reading (Ediger, 2001, ERIC, ED456410).

The learning community needs to think of diverse ways in which pupils and the teacher may help the former to attain more optimally. Pupils and the teacher need to evaluate the following in the reading curriculum, as an example, on a five point scale:

1. Is the classroom inviting for the reading of library books?
2. Do areas for large group committee work, and individual endeavours serve their purposes well for reading?

3. Is it easy to locate books you wish to read?
4. Is it easy to return books that you have read?
5. Are the written works of children displayed often for others to read?
6. Are there an ample number of books from different genera for pupils to read?
7. Are there ample library books available to read for different levels of reading ability?
8. Do you feel that much reading is encouraged in the classroom?
9. Is the level of noise in the classroom kept at a level whereby one can concentrate well on the task at hand?
10. Is ample time given for reading and writing in the classroom? (Ediger and Rao, 2000, 19).

REFERENCES

1. Ediger Marlow, and D. Bhaskara Rao (2000). *Teaching Mathematics Successfully*. New Delhi, India: Discovery Publishing House.
2. Ediger Marlow, and D. Bhaskara Rao (2001) *Teaching Science Successfully*. New Delhi: Discovery Publishing House.
3. Ediger, Marlow, and D. Bhaskara Rao (2001). *Teaching Social Studies Successfully*. New Delhi: Discovery Publishing House.

The Psychology of Improving Teaching Quality

Improving the quality of teaching in the classroom is a major goal of inservice education. The classroom teacher is the most important item or person involved to improve the curriculum. Each pupil must have the best education possible. This means that school administrators, supervisors of instruction, as well as classroom teachers need to be aware of needed improvements which should be made in teaching and learning situations. There are a plethora of ways available to improve the quality of instruction in the classroom. Each plan deserves adequate attention and indepth study to know in what direction the curriculum is to go. A vision of what should be is highly important for all involved in curriculum improvement. Tyler (1949) raised four questions which teachers and administrators should ask about the curriculum:

1. Which objectives should pupils achieve?
2. Which learning activities will assist pupils to achieve these objectives?
3. How should the curriculum be organised?
4. How should pupil achievement be evaluated?

These questions provide a frame work for inservice education of teachers. To improve the quality of teaching and learning situations, different types of inservice education need to be in the offing.

Styles of Leadership

It takes quality leadership to guide and direct a group of professionals to move forward in goal attainment. There are, basically, three leadership styles which may be used by leaders to help others in achieving, growing, and developing in a selected direction. The hierarchical leader tends to be rather directive in his/her leadership role. He/she generally has and uses a one way street of communication. The hierarchical leader knows what is wanted and communicates these ideas to teachers in a meeting, in bulletins, in memos, in conversation, as well as in other ways to force compliance to his/her line of thinking on an issue or trend. Instead of being an issue, there are no pros and cons, but a correct way exists in doing things. The right way is predetermined, prior to any faculty meeting, workshop, or inservice education programme. The details have been worked out ahead of time by the school supervisor or principal. These are to be communicated as absolutes to others. There is little or no room for discussion of ideas. The ideal for the hierarchical leader is to have teachers accept his/her commentary as factual content. This rules out debate, elaboration, or extending of presented ideas. Critical and creative thinking, as well as problem solving, are not emphasised in the curriculum.

A second leadership style is titled *democratic* and it provides participants a plethora of opportunities to discuss ideas presented by others. Ideas for curriculum improvement may come from anyone who will be affected by these decisions. Participants in any meeting know ahead of time what will be discussed and it appears in agenda form, several days before their consideration. The democratic leader invites input from faculty and parents. No one is to be left out who will be affected by decisions made. For each item on an agenda, there needs to be clarification of ideas presented at a meeting. Ideas are analysed for purposes of viewing pros and cons. Critical thinking is involved. New ideas are also sought within the framework of critical thinking. Thus, creative thinking can be involved. Novel and new ideas can then be forth coming when improving the curriculum! As creative ideas are presented, problem solving needs to occur in order to harmonize, if possible, the many ideas which are generated. The ultimate goal here to is to provide the best curriculum possible for pupils.

A third type if leadership is *laissez faire.* Laissez faire leadership is just the opposite of hierarchical styles. It stresses each individual making his/her own decisions pertaining to curriculum improvement. There is interaction among teachers if the individual so desires, but coordination and cooperation is lacking. Lassiez faire approaches in leadership can work, in degrees, if each teacher is highly knowledgeable, skilful in teaching, and works together with others, voluntarily, to develop a sequential curriculum of quality objectives, learning activities, and evaluation procedures. It is up to the teacher then to volunteer to work together with others for coordination in the school curriculum, or anarchy results in laissez faire leadership approaches (See Risko, et al., 134-144).

Leadership in curriculum development needs to focus on the following problems:

1. Which objectives is the school contemplating achieving with the involved budget?
2. Which criteria should be used to ascertain if the objectives have been achieved?

3. Who will be involved to determine if an acceptable standard has been used to determine goal attainment?
4. What costs were involved in achieving each goal?
5. Were the goals adequate in terms of acceptable standards in education as well as in community needs?
6. Should present programmes in education be changed or modified?
7. Were adequate resources available for goal attainment?
8. Were additional resources available for goals of instruction?
9. If additional resources are needed, how will this affect those who will share the burden in obtaining them?
10. How should present and future resources be used to achieve objectives efficiently and economically (Frohreich, 1983)?

The above named questions need to be considered carefully when instructional decisions are made. Quality leadership is necessary to make good curricular decisions.

Faculty Meetings

A long-standing method to use in curricular improvement is the faculty meeting in the local school. Faculty meetings can view the immediate as well as the here and now in analyzing the curriculum. Ongoing observations may be made by the teachers to notice changes which need to be made. School principals and supervisors need to view overall modifications which need to be made in the curriculum. Their observations may come from observational visits made to classrooms or from comments made by teachers to the principal and supervisor. An agenda can be made from these and other observational sources, for an ensuing faculty meeting. An agenda committee should be formed to accept and arrange these items. The agenda should be in the hands of faculty members, approximately, two days before the meeting so that each participant has adequate opportunities to study and think about solutions to these problems areas. Agenda items need to be analysed and discussed in-depth. If the agenda items are highly significant to all involved, then committees may be formed to study the item and report back to all faculty members. Input from all faculty members might well be in the offing to the committee report.

Within the faculty and committee meetings, there are definite criteria which need to be emphasised if successful interactions are to occur. These criteria include the following:

1. all members should contribute, but no one dominate the proceedings.
2. each member should respect the thinking of others. No minimizing or ridiculing of others should be in the offing.
3. interrupting the contributions of others must be avoided.
4. ideas should circulate within the discussion and not flow between two members consistently.
5. positive attitudes and good human relations should be practiced.
6. committee members should be adequately prepared for each meeting. Doing one's homework is salient.
7. ideas need to be presented clearly and succinctly.
8. committee members should feel free to ask for clarification of an idea which is not understood.

9. thorough discussion of each agenda item is important. Individuals, however, should not get bogged down on minutia.

10. careful minutes should be kept of each meeting and the contents presented to a total group such as the faculty of a school (Ediger and Rao, Chapter Seven, 2003).

The Workshop

A workshop might involve more than one school in a district. The workshop has selected items planned prior to its first session such as the place, theme, time durations, library, consultant assistance, theme, and speakers. Otherwise, selected items are planned within the workshop large group session such as identification of problem areas to be considered within the framework of the theme. Participants may choose which problem area to work on. Committee progress reports should be made at selected intervals to the large group. Individual endeavours should also be a part of the total workshop. Each teacher might well have a question for which answers need to be sought. He/she may then work by the self in answer seeking. The library contains resources which should be excellent to use in seeking answers to problems and questions.

Participants in the workshop need to try out solutions and answers in teaching and learning situations. The results of each tryout should be available to workshop participants. Recommendations for modification to the try out should also be a part of the reporting process. Feedback to what has been tried out in the classroom is must (Ediger, 1988, Chapter Thirteen).

Parental involvement in workshops is salient. The need for parents to be invited to attend and participate in workshops is important. Parents can certainly assist pupils to achieve well in school. These needs to be quality parental involvement. The following are levels of parental involvement:

1. parents receiving information, in a variety of ways, from the school to improve parenting procedures.
2. quality methods of communicating between parents and the school being in evidence.
3. volunteering to help pupils at home with school work.
4. involvement in parent/teacher organisations in decision making roles.
5. parents securing assistance from community organisations to help pupils to do better in school (Epstein, 1995).

Parental involvement in a constructive way is important when working toward more optimal pupil achievement in school. They need to be invited and participate in school sponsored workshops.

To achieve well in workshops, participants need to be aware of reasons why innovations fail in duration. Strength of leadership in the curriculum might be lacking in motivating teachers. Participants lack purpose or agreement for making vital changes. Inadequate or no funding is available to keep an innovation progressing. An innovation may be costly. The innovation might fall apart due to rapid turnover of teachers in the school setting. Continuity in making curriculum changes improves sequential pupil learning. School wide commitment and participation needs encouragement when attempting to make curricular changes.

Adopting An Entirely New Programme

Sometimes, a public school adopts an entirely new programme for instruction such as in reading. The old reading programme then is discarded and the completely new replacement is brought in to teaching and learning situations. Hopefully, teachers will have indepth studied the replacement programme and agree to its implementation. Otherwise, it can be quite destabilizing to do away completely with the known programme and replace it with an entirely new reading curriculum. Quality leadership is highly necessary to adopt a completely new curriculum. Generally, a previous programme is gradually phased out or the previous curriculum is modified, such as in the faculty meeting or workshop approach in curricular improvement. Thus, for example, individualised reading is brought into the reading curriculum and the use of basal readers remain. Both individualised reading and basals are used simultaneously in reading instruction. Basals, for example, gradually may then be replaced with individualised reading.

If, however, individualised reading is completely replaced with one which has an opposite philosophy of instruction, the feelings of teachers might be quite destabilizing. Thus if Reading Mastery readers replace individualised reading at one time, there will tend to be feelings of much anxiety and uncertainty among teachers. Why? Individualised reading is completely open ended in which each pupil selects a library book to read silently. A conference with the teacher follows the silent reading whereby the teacher raises questions covering the completed silent reading of the library book. Here, the teacher evaluates comprehension skills of the pupil. The child's feelings toward reading might also be assessed. Also, it is good to appraise the pupil's oral reading fluency to notice fluency in the pupil's ability to read. Proficiency in the sue of word attack skills needs careful observation by the teacher. The teacher may record necessary information from the conference and make comparisons of the same pupil with the next ensuing conference.

Reading Mastery readers, published by Science Research Associates (SRA) and also known as Distar, are highly scripted and contain precise text for teachers to use in reading instruction. There is little room for teacher creativity in using these readers. Reading Mastery is used by pupils who face difficulties in learning to read. It is tightly sequenced in phonics instruction and contains a highly controlled vocabulary. Words individually may be contrived to rhyme with other words, even though nonsense syllables are used. Thus, the word "sun" has meaningful rhyming words such as bun, run, fun, gun, pun. However, there are syllables which pattern, but are not meaningful words such as zun, lun, mun, yun. Pupils are to hear likenesses and differences in sounds when the initial consonant is changed, but the rest of word or syllable patterns in terms of rhyme. Pupils are to pay very close attention to what is taught by looking at the print and not be distracted by objects or by others in the group setting. The teacher tightly controls what is taught as well methodology used, as presented in the manual. He/she is very directive in having pupils focus attention upon what is being taught and learned. In a tightly scripted reading programme, the objectives are stated in measurable terms in that either a child does/does not achieve the stated ordered objectives as a result of instruction. Reinforcement techniques are commonly used in that each pupil is rewarded with extrinsic rewards when responding correctly to a teacher's directions in teaching reading. The pupils then respond to the teacher's directions in learning. Since the Reading Mastery instructional programme is quite different from what was used previously such as individualised reading, for example, inservice education for teachers would definitely be needed. This is an example of replacing a programme of reading instruction from what was to a completely new plan of teaching and learning.

When a completely new curriculum is brought in to replace the old, teachers need to buy into the new reading programme. Thus, teachers.

1. have read articles on and listened to discussions pertaining to the new curriculum?
2. have asked questions about the new curriculum and interacted with the ideas presented?
3. have examined materials of instruction pertaining to the ensuing programme of instruction?
4. have experienced a workshop on teaching the new programme of instruction?
5. have reached favourably to the new programme?
6. have strong beliefs in favouring a tightly developed sequence in reading instruction?
7. have inherent beliefs in the teacher controlling the teaching situation, with no pupil input along the way?
8. have knowledge, skills, and attitudes toward a curriculum which emphasizes the imparting of information within pupils?
9. have beliefs pertaining to all knowledge acquired is measurable?
10. have beliefs that inherent philosophies of reading instruction are clear cut and that scientific methods of instruction should be used? (See also, Paris, 2002).

Inservice Education for Teachers

With the increasingly common situation of using computers in the classroom setting, it might be wise for teachers to experience assistance in becoming more sophisticated in the use of technology. If Accelerated Readers (AR) are to be used in reading instruction, there are selected things which teachers need to learn. The AR computer system provides more than 22,000 different fiction and non-fiction books on different reading levels. Pupils then choose a book to read on their individual reading level. After reading the contents, the pupil takes a computerised test involving multiple choice test items. The test measures the pupil's comprehension from reading the story. Immediately, receives feedback pertaining to his/her score as well as questions on incorrectly answered questions. The computer keep record of the pupil's accumulated test scores in order to be eligible to receive an earned prize. Computer results provide information to the teacher in tracking the pupil's total achievement such as the number of books read, number of questions answered correctly, and the number of points earned from test results (Cuddeback and Ceprano, 2002).

In an inservice programme of education to use AR readers, teachers need to be able to

1. assist pupils in the mechanics of computer use in order to increase proficiency in learner reading.
2. use a management system to monitor each pupil's progress in reading.
3. explain the philosophy and psychology of computer use in reading instruction.
4. communicate research results on using computers in teaching reading, especially the Accelerated Reader.
5. develop a rationale in using extrinsic motivation in reading instruction, as well as explain attempts in moving pupils to higher levels of cognition when taking in subject matter via computer use.

Depending upon present teacher competency in computer use, inservice education will need to be provided to take care of individual needs to implement AR instruction. AR provides opportunities for pupils to achieve individually at an optimal level. Each pupil receives feedback on how well he/she did on tests pertaining to content read. The pupil can move forward at his/her own optimal rate and speed in reading. He/she may choose what to read sequentially, including the complexity level of the chosen book. The computerised management system keeps track of pupil progress in each designated area of reading. The teaching is then better able to provide assistance to pupils individually since computerised tests and scoring are used along with the tracking of the complexity level of library books read.

There are definite problems which need amelioration in pupil reading. These include

1. mispronounciation of words.
2. omitting words while reading.
3. not paying attention to punctuation marks.
4. hesitating on selected words being read.
5. failure to associate graphemes with phonemes when there is consistency between symbol and sound.
6. too much stress placed on phonics when there is a lack of consistency between grapheme and phoneme.
7. insufficient attention paid to thought units when reading subject matter.
8. a lack of attention paid to holism, such as when the pupil segments words into syllables when this is not needed.
9. too much attention paid to holism in reading. The pupil needs to read words and sentences, more carefully, so that accuracy is involved in comprehension (Ediger and Rao, 2003, 141).

There are diverse kinds of comprehension which pupils need to develop skill in, when reading ideas. These include:

1. reading important facts.
2. reading to skim subject matter.
3. reading to follow directions.
4. reading to develop generalisations.
5. reading for a main idea.
6. reading to think critically.
7. reading to think creatively.
8. reading to solve problems.
9. reading for enjoyment.
10. reading to determine cause and effect (Ediger and Rao, 2003, 142).

The above named skills are important for pupils to achieve and apply in different reading situations. Each skill is clearly different from the others and needs to be stressed within teaching and learning situations.

State Mandated Standards

Most states in the union have developed mandated objectives for pupil attainment. These objectives are available as benchmarks for teacher use in teaching pupils. State mandated tests should be aligned with the their objectives of instruction. Validity is involved if the tests measure what is stated in the objectives. Pilot studies should be conducted by each state to take out kinks within their test. Reliability is in evidence when, in the pilot study, pupils receive the same/similar test score from repeated testing. Reliability may then be test/retest, alternative forms, and/or split half. Faculty meetings and workshops may be conducted to strengthen teachers teaching so that pupils achieve ends, such as the state mandated objectives of instruction (See also, Richard, September 4, 2002).

REFERENCES

1. Cuddeback, Meghan, and Maria A. Ceprano (2002), *"The use of Accelerated Reader with Emergent Readers,"* Reading Improvement, 39(2), 89-95.
2. Ediger, Marlow, and D. Bhaskara Rao (2003), *Improving School Administration.* New Delhi, India: Discovery Publishing House, 141 and 142.
3. Ediger, Marlow, and D. Bhaskara Rao (2003), *Language Arts Curriculum.* New Delhi, India: Discovery Publishing House, Chapter Thirteen.
4. Ediger, Marlow (1988), *The Elementary Curriculum,* 2nd Edition. Kirksville, Missouri: Simpson Publishing Company, Chapter Seven.
5. Epstein, Joyce (1995), *"School/Family/Community Partnerships,"* Phi Delta Kappan, 76: 704.
6. Friedrich, L.E. (1983), *"The School Budgeting Cycle,"* Winneconne, Wisconsin.
7. Paris, Scott (2002), *"Centre for Improvement of Early Reading Achievement,"* Reading Teacher, 55(2), 170.
8. Richard, Alan (September 4, 2002), *Florida Sees Surge in Use of Vouchers,"* Education Week, 1, 34.
9. Risko, Virginia J., et al. (2002), *"Preparing Teachers for Reflective Practice:"* Intentions, Contradictions, and Possibilities," Language Arts, 82(2), 134-144.
10. Tyler, Ralph (1949), *Basic Principles of Curriculum Construction.* Chicago: University of Chicago Press.

The Psychology of Reading Instruction

The teacher needs to be well versed in the teaching of reading. There is content to read in each curriculum area regardless of the grade level taught. There also are clearly differentiated programme of instruction. Each is based on a selected psychological school of thought. Educators need to study and analyze each school of thought to see where it would fit into a quality programme of instruction. Each programme of instruction needs to meet needs of pupils. Meeting needs is a sound way of thinking about the curriculum. Rather than emphasizing one traditional plan of teaching, the teacher needs to study and analyze pupil's curricular achievement to see what fits into the learner's repertoire of skills and knowledge. For example, it is the pupil who needs to be taught to read and not emphasis being placed upon tradition, or authoritarian beliefs. The materials and methods of instruction should harmonize with what would assist pupils to achieve optimally in reading.

Basal Reading Instruction

The use of carefully chosen basal readers has a set of beliefs which encourages their use. They have been chosen for publication by a commercial company and are generally written and edited by a select set of reading specialists.

Basals have an accompanying manual for teachers to use in choosing objectives, learning opportunities, and evaluation techniques. These may be used en toto or in part, as the teacher chooses. The manual may be good for beginning teachers to use; later the more experienced teacher needs to be increasingly creative in developing his/her own reading curriculum to meet pupil needs. There are dangers in using the manual religiously, year after school year, which can make for a stultifying reading curriculum.

The teacher needs to group pupils appropriately when using the basal reader for instructional purposes. Pupils should experience flexible grouping, heterogeneously or homogeneously, depending upon what would help the individual child to optimize achievement. Thus, the content read should not be too easy which can make for boredom or a lack of interest, nor should it be too complex making for pupil failure. There needs be a starting point in reading for each pupil where he/she is developing optimally an sequentially. Each pupil needs to achieve as much as personal abilities permit, and yet be successful in learning to read as well as possible (See also Vacca, 2002).

Items which would make the basal more developmental for pupils are the following:

1. since basals are written for a group of grade level pupils in a classroom, the teacher needs to individualize instruction so that each pupil might benefit as much as possible from the textbook.
2. teachers should use the manual creatively so that the best ideas possible are used for teaching and learning in reading. Ideas can then be chosen from the manual, from the teacher's repertoire and from quality research in the teaching of reading.
3. individual endeavours, committee work, and large group instruction may be used as needed in the

instructional arena. In large group instruction, the teacher may introduce new words and their contextual meanings, word recognition techniques, and build background information within pupils for reading the ensuing selection. Committee work might involve four pupils, for example, to discuss the completed reading selection. Individualised instruction provides opportunities for a learner to pursue related projects and activities.

4. active involvement of pupils is necessary so that pupils are carefully attending to ongoing instruction. This might well mean small group or individual instruction.

5. each group should be given assistance as needed. Teacher aides are necessary to assist pupils as needed. They work with the supervision of he regular teacher. Retired teachers, in the community, are glad to provide time in the regular classroom by listening to children read orally and check comprehension, among other tasks.

6. adequate time should be given to followup activities after pupils have read a given selection. To indicate what has been comprehended through reading, pupils individually or collectively may do an art project such as a mural, a pencil sketch, à construction activity, and/or a dramatisation.

7. pupils need to have adequate opportunities to discuss content read. Not only can depth learning be stressed here, but also skills in communicating ideas.

8. higher levels of cognition must be stressed. These include critical thinking whereby the pupil learns to analyze subject matter to separate fact from opinion, reality versus fantasy, as well the accurate

from the inaccurate. Creative thinking by pupils is salient. The learner then develops novel, unique ideas pertaining to the selection read. Problems solving is also salient in that pupils need to identify and solve problems from reading subject matter. A curious person is needed in the reading arena.

9. phonics instruction should only be given when a pupil needs these learnings to identify unknown words. Phonics should not be taught for the sake of doing so, but to guide proficiency in reading words more fluently to increase comprehension. Phonics should not be taught since it is in the traditional reading curriculum, but their acknowledgment is based on analysis and remediation of problems in reading instruction. The individual child is the focal point of teaching and learning, not external sources of determining objectives of instruction. Sound/symbol relationships need be consistent for phonics instruction to be successful. Syllabication skills also should be taught when each is commonly used in reading and assists the child to read better. Knowing how to divide unknown words into syllables is salient if a pupil can benefit from these learnings and can identify words more proficiently.

10. context cludes should be taught as the need arises for the pupil to recognize unknown words. It is the best word recognition technique available to assist pupils in identifying the unknown. Reading skills should not be taught due to their being indicated for lesson preparation in the manual of the basal reader, but rather are based on individual pupil diagnosis and remediation (Ediger and Rao, 2000, Chapter Six).

Individualised Reading

Individualised reading experts advocate the use of library books, rather than basals in teaching and learning situations. With individualised reading, the pupil chooses the library book to read with intrinsic interests involved. Here, the beliefs are that a pupil is in the best position to determine what to read since the subject matter in the chosen library book tends to be appealing. The level of complexity of a selected book harmonizes with the instructional level of reading. In the instructional reading level, the pupil is able, generally, to identify, approximately, 95 per cent of the running words read. He/she is also able to answer at least 75 per cent of the questions raised covering content from the library book chosen for reading. Interest is a powerful factor in pupils liking and learning to read. The individual pupil, alone, selects and reads the self chosen library book.

A good selection of library books needs to be on hand for reading. Books need to be available which meet personal needs of pupils and are written on diverse genres. They might be briefly introduced with bulletin board displays or introduced orally to encourage pupil reading, depending upon time available. Following the reading of a library book, the pupil may have a conference with the teacher to assess comprehension and reading skills (See McKeown, et al., 1992).

Items which need to be emphasised in individualised reading include the following:

1. each pupil needs to have the freedom the choose a library book to read which is interesting. The teacher steps in for book selection if a child cannot settle down with making a choice. Here, the teacher may choose a library book suitable for the learner.

2. the learning environment needs to have a quietness which promotes the reading process(es).

3. the teacher needs to arrange his/her schedule to be available for conferences. Alternatives may be offered with a pupil writing a report on a completed reading of a library book. Standards for writing the report need to be clarified with learners. Excellent readers may not need to have a conference each time a book has been completed in reading. The teacher will need to make adjustments so that as much as possible, conferences can be held with each pupil, following the reading of a library book. The teacher needs to briefly record the outcomes of the conference. Comparisons might then be made with the next sequential conference for each pupil.

4. pupils should be given opportunities to do an alternative evaluation such as using non-verbal means including drawing an illustration of major ideas read from a library book.

5. most reading specialists say that reading is its very own reward. Intrinsic motivation is then being advocated. Others may believe that extrinsic rewards should be in the offing such as small, inexpensive prizes given for a pupil reading a certain numbers of library books.

6. the teacher needs to think of a variety of approaches to motivate pupil reading of library books, such as a committee sharing contents of library books completed.

7. an approach should be used to assist pupils with the pronunciation of unknown words. Perhaps, the teacher's aide or a good reader can do the word pronunciation for those who are stuck in reading a particular word.

8. a teacher's aide could listen in to sequential conferences conducted by the teacher of pupil progress. The aide may then date and record the salient ideas from the conference. This makes it so the teacher could handle more conferences effectively. The aide, if he/she is a good reader, should read aloud to pupils during story time.
9. pupils need to be as accountable as individual maturity levels permit. The pupil then is in charge of learning opportunities being pursued. Pupil ownership of the curriculum is necessary if they are to develop well intrinsically with good attitudes toward learning.
10. the effectiveness of the individualised reading programme needs continuous evaluation with feedback from learners being used to make improvements (See Saunders, 1999).

A parallel to individualised reading is sustained silent reading (SSR). Here, too, the pupil chooses the sequential library books to read. However, there is no time given for conferences after a library book has been completed in reading. Enjoyment and encouragement of reading are major goals in SSR. Hopefully, in an environment of complete relaxation, the pupil seeks, selects, and reads a quality library book. Time is made available in the school schedule for SSR, a very informal time for reading. In some schools, everyone reads at the designated SSR time, including all teachers, support personnel, custodians, and school administrators. The point being that all pupils need to see adults reading books also. This is a model for children. Probably, if the teacher in the classroom reads during SSR time, this should be an adequate adult model for pupils to view. Then, too, most pupils would not be able to see a custodian read. The custodian has a plethora of responsibilities to fulfil and maintain a quality, clean school environment.

Pupils are responsible for selecting their own materials to read. They need to use the entire time for SSR when the schedule calls for it. Busy readers with self selected reading materials are musts! The interest factor can be very high in reading when pupils do the choosing of what to read. They order their own learnings when choosing sequential library books to read. In an informal setting such as in SSR, pupils should feel very relaxed to read at their own unique optimal rates of speed. The psychology of reading certainly is there when SSR is in evidence in the classroom setting (See, Giorgas, 1999).

Teachers need to work with parents in suggesting ways of helping pupils learn. Thus, for example, parents should read aloud selected library books which fill the bill in meeting pupil needs. Schools should provide parents a listing of library books to read to their offspring in the home setting. Tips on and for successful home reading practices should be included, such as reading with enthusiasm, having eye contact with the child, showing related illustrations in the library book, as well as using appropriate stress, pitch, and intonation as the read aloud continues.

Using Big Book Approaches

Big Book procedures in teaching should emphasize that all pupils, being taught, need to see the illustrations and printed script clearly from where they are seated. The teacher provides background information for the ensuing reading lesson. Pupils might then connect the previous with the new learnings. After providing background information, which includes discussing the illustrations embedded in the script, the teacher reads aloud to pupils by pointing to each sequential word. Pupils need to observe the script carefully as the read aloud continues. Observing carefully what the teacher reads aloud, as he/she points to the words, assists learners to increase their basic sight vocabulary. The rereading consists of learners reading together with the teacher, as the words are pointed to again. Regarding may occur as frequently as desired. Many times children like to reread subject matter due to feelings of success in mastering new words as well as in understanding the background information more thoroughly.

Big Book procedures might be used on any grade level. It can be a good way to teach primary grade pupils in reading. There are older children who fail to develop an adequate basic sight vocabulary, but can do so with the teacher pointing to new words as ensuing reading lessons progress, using the Big Book approach (Ediger, 2002, 69-70).

Big Book approaches, to make for optimal learner progress in methods of teaching, should emphasize the following pointers:

1. selecting content which appeals to pupils. Obtaining pupil attention is vital.
2. building ample background information for pupils prior to their reading the printed script, so that the new content to be read is sequential and is understood.
3. pronouncing words clearly and pointing to each word being read aloud, contextually.
4. having as much eye contact with pupils as possible to make reading personal.
5. helping pupils develop an adequate basic sight vocabulary by reading and rereading the printed script meticulously.
6. using proper intonation, as a model, so that pupils learn to pronounce words properly.
7. being certain that all being taught from the Big Book can see the illustrations clearly as well as the printed script therein.

8. evaluating pupil achievement carefully to notice if new, abstract words are being mastered, as well as comprehension being improved upon, over that of previous times.
9. involving pupils in ascertaining what needs additional stress in the Big Book approach in reading instruction.
10. assessing sequence in reading stories in Big Books. The teacher needs to determine if related learnings on phonics should be in the offing to improve pupil comprehension (Crawley, S., and K. Merritt, 2000).

A Controlled Vocabulary

Readers containing a controlled vocabulary have advantages and disadvantages, but that is true of many plans of teaching and learning. The controlled vocabulary made it so that pupils in these basals would meet up with a few new words per page of printed content. The rest of the printed page for primary age pupils, in particular, would have the repeat of important words. In other words, the authors controlled how many new words would be emphasised per page so that it would not be overwhelming for the reader. Too many new words introduced per page might well frustrate any reader. One guideline used for choosing expository books for classroom use, as well as for individual reading, is to not overdo new words brought into any reading selection. There needs to be a balance between new words on a page of print for young readers, in particular, and review or practice of previous words encountered. If more than five per cent of the words encountered by a reader are unknown words, the tendency will be for that book to be too complex for pupil reading. A strong interest in a piece of written work can make it so that the "more then five per cent" level may be modified. It is important to have successful readers. There is, generally, too much in life which is frustrating without planning for a lack of pupil success in learning. Success tends to motivate pupils for increased achievement. If a person has experienced too much of failure, the chances are that he/she will tend to give up on life and its opportunities (Ediger, 2001, ERIC, 456410).

Pointers to stress by the teacher in using a controlled vocabulary text in making for successful readers include the following:

1. observe which pupils need to thoroughly controlled vocabulary as compared to those who become independent readers sooner. The latter group could, perhaps, read more library books as well as stay on for the controlled vocabulary reading programme, as needed. There are a plethora of decisions which need to be made by the teacher.
2. have pupils read the controlled vocabulary sections with enthusiasm. Vibrant reading is necessary in all oral reading, be it by pupils, by parents, or by the teacher. The models presented by the teacher and by pupils in read alouds should emphasise spontaneity and creativity, not dullness or routine procedures.
3. coach pupils to read selected stories in shorter periods of time since learners individually reveal increased mastery of words encountered. Not all sections or stories are of the same/similar complexity within a controlled reader. The teacher always needs to observe and study pupils to notice needs that exist in children becoming successful readers. With success, the self concept is developed in a positive manner.
4. reward pupils verbally when increased success in reading has been encountered. Esteem needs

might then be met. Each pupil has contributions to make and these must be recognised by the teacher and pupils.

5. plan with pupils what needs to be stressed more so, in the ongoing reading programme. Parental input might also be valuable when parent/teacher conferences are held (Ediger, 2001, ERIC, 455496).

Linguistic Programmes of Reading Instruction

There are a plethora of linguistic procedures in the teaching of reading. The approaches of Leonard Bloomfield and Charles Fries will be discussed as to their philosophy and psychology of linguistic reading instruction. Both emphasised a patterns approach in the teaching of reading. There are selected word patterns which may be used to illustrate their thinking. For example, pupils initially might well experiment with the following patterns in readings: an, ban, can, fan, man, ran, tan, van. Some meaningful sentences may be written to show a linguistic approach in reading instruction from the above words such as in the following: man can fan. Each word patterns with the other in rhyme as well as in correct spelling. It is not the best way to write this sentence, but it does illustrate structure in a patterning approach, according to linguists Bloomfield and Fries.

Meaning is lacking when attempting to write sentences with word patterns. However, it does pay attention to certain elements such as changing an initial consonant and a new word results such as changing the letter "m" in "man" to the letter "c" making for a new word "can."

Several basal spelling textbooks use linguistic procedures in having pupils learn to spell words. The pattern may be represented by changing an initial consonant of a word to secure a new word—tan, ban. The ending letter, too, may be changed to obtain a new word such as: tan, tab. Medial letters, also, may be changed to come up with a different word—tan, tin. There are patterns involved when adding a silent letter "e" to a word and the word changes its vowel sound from being a short sound to a long vowel sound: can, cane. Pupils may play with words to notice which pattern and which do not: tan, tane. The latter is not a meaningful word. There, of course, are limitations to the pattering approach. But, there are selected features which do assist pupils to observe patterns in words. Then, too, pupils may notice where a lack of relationship exists between symbol and sound, such as: through, threw, slough, blue, soon, dune. Pupils might then notice inconsistencies in spelling involving the "oo" sound as in "moon." The author suggests these words, of course, be learned by pupils in word recognition as sight words. There are a plethora of ways available to spell vowel sounds such as for the letter "a." The following words contain the letter "a" and yet each has a different grapheme/phoneme relationship: ran, rain, rate, rare, about.

Linguists have made a plethora of contributions when writing sentence patterns, in written discourse, such as:

- the subject/predicate pattern.
- the subject/predicate, direct object pattern.
- the subject/predicate/indirect object, direct object pattern.
- the subject/predicate (linking verb), predicate adjective pattern.
- the subject/predicate/predicate noun pattern (Tiedt, 1983).

With a developmental knowledge of sentence patterns, pupils may vary these to improve writing quality. Linguistic procedures of instruction may be improved upon by.

1. its appropriate use in spelling and reading, and by recognising its limitations.

2. its use might assist pupils to study and learn about the structure of the English language. Other languages have their very own structure and patterns. A developmental approach needs to be used in teaching and learning situations involving a linguistic approach. Learnings then should harmonize with pupils acquiring new achievable objectives. Failure to achieve on the pupil's part violates rules pertaining to the following:

1. pupils developing a good self concept.
2. pupils achieving self esteem.
3. pupils learning sequential content and skills.
4. pupils becoming motivated individuals.
5. pupils becoming reflective learners (Douillard, 2002).

REFERENCES

1. Crawley, S., and K. Merritt (2000), *Remediating Reading Difficulties.* Boston: Mc Graw Hill.
2. Douillad, Kim (2002), *"Going Past Done: Creating Time for Reflection in the Classroom,"* Language Arts, 80(2), 92-99.
3. Ediger, Marlow (2002), *"Improving Spelling,"* Reading Improvement, 39(2), 69-70.
4. Ediger, Marlow, and D. Bhaskara Rao (2000), *Teaching Reading Successfully.* New Delhi, India: Discovery Publishing House, Chapter Six.
5. Ediger, Marlow (2001), *"Analyzing Student Difficulties in Reading,"* ERIC, 456410.
6. Ediger, Marlow (2001), *"Reading and the Curriculum,"* ERIC, 455496.
7. Giorigs, C. (1999), *The Power of Reading Picture Books Aloud to Secondary Students,"* The Clearing House, 73, 51-53.
8. Mc Keown, M.G., et al., (1992), *"The Contribution of Prior Knowledge and Coherent Text to Comprehension,"* Reading Research Quarterly, 27, 79-93.

9. Saunders, S. (1999), "*Look and Learn: Using Picture Books in Grades Five through Eight*. Portsmouth, New Hampshire: Heinemann.

10. Tiedt, Iris M. (1983), *The Language Arts Handbook*. Englewood Cliffs, New Jersey: Prentice-Hall, Inc., Chapter Eleven.

11. Vacca, Richard T. (2002), "*From Efficient Decoders to Strategic Readers*," Educational Leadership, 60(3), 6-11.

Grouping and Organising for Instruction

There are a plethora of concerns involved when pupils are placed into groups for teaching and learning purposes. Each concern addresses a different problem. Pupils differ from each other in numerous ways. These differences include ability levels, interests possessed, purposes involved in learning, motivation and energy levels for achieving. The group a pupil is placed in should assist him/her to attain as optimally as possible. Perhaps, flexibility is a key term to emphasize when grouping pupils for instruction since a pupil might be in a different group for one academic area as compared to another due to strengths possessed (See Gunning, Chapter Eleven).

Grouping for Basal Reading Instruction

With the use of a basal textbook, the teacher needs to determine under which plan of grouping for instruction, the child will do best. The entire class may be taught together when the teacher introduces new words which pupils will encounter in the ensuing reading selection from the basal. The new words to be read need to be printed in neat, manuscript letters on the chalkboard. Each pupil should be able to see the words clearly. The teacher with pupils then may go over the identification and pronunciation of these words until mastery has occurred. Phonics or sounds/symbol relations in the new words may be stressed as needed. Pupils also need to know the contextual meaning for each word as it is used in the text. Discussing the illustrations in the text assists pupils to further develop background information for reading from the ensuing content. Next, there should be questions which pupils might have raised by this time, or the teacher may identify selected questions. These questions can be answered by pupils when reading from the basal textbook. These followup activities might be quite varied. Pupils may wish to show comprehension in different ways such as:

1. drawing one or more illustrations to reveal comprehension.
2. three members in class developing a mural or collage to indicate what has been learned from reading.
3. constructing an object, individually or collectively to show major ideas read.
4. telling orally about main concepts read in the reading selection.
5. dramatizing collaboratively that which was acquired through reading (Ediger and Rao, 2000, Chapter Twenty-two).

Generally, pupils are grouped heterogeneously when basal texts are used in teaching. However, there are teachers who divide the total group in the classroom into three subgroups based on ability. This would then be called homogenous grouping. Negative names should not be used to identify which group a pupil is in. Each pupil needs to be respected and accepted. The three groups may have different basal readers such as those being the most difficult to read, those of lesser difficulty, and the third group would have the easiest text to read. They may also be in different places within the basal. These texts are chosen based on the developmental level of each child. The new words are listed on the chalkboard for pupil viewing. Contextual meanings for each word are developed as they will be read in the textbook. The related illustrations in the text are discussed to build pupil background information for reading the ensuing subject matter. Questions will be raised by pupils and/or the teacher for which content being read might well supply needed answers. Pupils then read silently the subject matter contained in the story, after which a discussion should follow to extend and enrich learnings gained from reading in each of the three homogeneously grouped sets of pupils.

Heterogeneous versus homogeneously grouped pupils has long been an issue in education. The author takes the point of view that both can be emphasised depending upon needs of the involved pupils. The teacher needs to determine under which conditions do pupils achieve more optimally. Thus, in a follow up activity following reading and discussing of subject matter read, pupils may work on a related project, heterogeneously (mixed achievement levels) or homogeneously grouped based on ability.

Pupils reading from a basal text can be stressed in all academic areas and thus emphasize reading across the curriculum.

Advantages given for heterogeneous grouping are the following:

1. Democracy is in evidence when pupils who possess diverse differences are not regregated from each other, but have ample chances to learn from each other, as well as develop positive attitudes to others.
2. Society emphasizes that individuals interact with each other regardless of capacity and achievement

levels. Thus, the school setting must implement strategies in which individuals learn to live together harmoniously with others regardless of capacity traits possessed differ from each other in a plethora of ways.

Advantages given for homogeneous grouping are the following:

1. it is easier in planning to teach a uniform group of achievers instead of trying to teach a set of pupils where the range of achievement is great indeed.

2. it is true that pupils may challenge each other by being more uniform in achievement. It is feasible to have somewhat alike achievers motivate each other by example. Generally, with heterogeneously grouped pupils, the lowest member cannot possibly keep up and be challenged by top achieves (See, Lieu, 2000).

Reading from Library Books

Instead of using the basal or together with basal textbook use in the curriculum, pupils might read library books. With the us of library books, individualised reading is being emphasised. Each pupil chooses a library book to read, based on his/her reading level and on the topic preferred. Thus, there needs to be available an adequate number of library books on different reading levels and on different topics to provide for individual differences. The pupil is the chooser. After completing the reading of a library book, the pupil may have a conference with the teacher to ascertain pupil comprehension and the quality of oral reading. The teacher may record observations made and compare earlier with later conferences to ascertain pupil achievement. When using individualised reading exclusively, there are no problems in grouping pupils for instruction.

Each is reading a different library book based own his/ her very on interest and achievement level.

In each academic area, library books may be read instead of reading from the basal text Thus, in a science/ social studies unit of study such as "The Changing Surface of the Earth," each pupil may select a library book to read on that topic and join in on the discussion for each day's lesson. Related projects may be developed pertaining to that unit of study, either individually or collectively such as making a model volcano to understand the concept of "volcanic eruptions" more thoroughly. If a committee of pupils works collaboratively on a project, then either heterogeneous or homogeneous grouping may be stressed. The teacher needs to be skilled in using diverse kinds of grouping procedures. There should be opportunities for pupils to learn from each other in both heterogeneously grouped and homogeneously grouped learners. Whole group, small groups, and individuals endeavours make it necessary for the teacher to think which kind of grouping, heterogeneously or homogeneously, should pupils experience to achieve as optimally as possible (See Moss and Hendershot, 2002).

In school and in society, individuals interact with those of similar reading ability levels as well as when a mixed achievement level of individuals is in the offing.

Multi-age Grouping

Multi-grade grouping is practiced, generally, if a teacher teachers a combination room of third and fourth graders. Here, pupils may be grouped heterogeneously by teaching the third grades separately from the fourth graders. There will generally be a wide range of achievement in each grade. Thus, the third graders may achieve in reading from the first to the fifth grade, whereas the fourth graders may read from the second to the sixth grade levels in reading achievement.

There are combination room teachers who group pupils into three homogeneously grouped sets of learners. In the top reading group, there will be both third and fourth graders. This would be true, too, for the average, as well as slowest achievers.

Pupils may well vary from each other in terms of how well they achieve in each academic area. Thus, a pupil may be in the top group in reading, but somewhat towards the average in mathematics. Selected pupils may also achieve toward the top in all academic areas. Or a pupil may achieve at the lowest level in all academic disciplines. Judgments need to be made by the teacher in terms of how often to group homogeneously for reading instruction only, or for each of the different academic areas including mathematics and science. There could be many groups taught in this case. With heterogeneous grouping in combination rooms, third graders being taught separately from fourth graders will automatically tend to make for heterogeneous grouping as will be true for fourth graders being taught in a group (Ediger and Rao, 2001).

Pupils in Transition Rooms

In some schools where pupils do not do passing work for a specific grade level, a transition room of learners may be formed. Pupils then who have done failing work on a grade level may be passed on to the next grade level in order to stay with their peers. However, these pupils will be given extra assistance and help to make up for identified deficiencies. It may be that a retired teacher can give this extra assistance on the next grade level. It could be that the transition room pupils receive tutoring before or after school. Peer teaching, when desirable, may be implemented to assist those deemed to lack needed knowledge and skills. Summer school is a good time, too, for transition pupils to receive needed assistance. Selected schools have even emphasised Saturday morning class time for those deemed insufficient in achievement. Might pupils then spend too much time in school work? The goal for transition room pupils is to catch up with what are considered to be realistic goals. In one school where the author supervised university student teachers, the board of education had adopted a ruling that pupils who did not complete classroom assignments would need to do so after school. Parents, then, would pick up their offspring after classroom work had been completed (Ediger, 1988, Chapter Eight).

Team Teaching and Grouping for Instruction

There are several plans of team teaching. However, most plans boil down to the following:

1. two or more teachers plan together to teach a given set of pupils. The team than cooperatively chooses the objectives, learning opportunities, and the assessment procedures.

2. the team has one teacher whose strengths are the greatest to teach a single lesson for large group instruction. The other teacher(s), take their turn teaching in large group instruction. They observe and help pupils stay on task during large group instruction.

3. smaller groups or committees follow with clarification of ideas and skills taught in large group instruction. Learnings are also extended, as well as taught in depth. Follow up instruction emphasizes diagnosis and remediation of pupil needs.

4. individual endeavours stress pupils doing something purposefully such as doing a project relating to the large or small group sessions.

5. team members evaluate pupil achievement in a conference setting in which each member has

contributions to make in improving the curriculum for pupils individually (See Gordan).

Cooperation and harmony among team teaching members are vital for collaborative endeavours to function successfully. The team instead of individuals planning the curriculum makes for a new perspective in teaching. Members may well learn from each other in planning for instruction as well as when observing the quality of instruction from actual teaching. In large and small group instruction, pupils may be grouped heterogeneously or homogeneously when being taught by a teaching team. Advocates of team teaching stress that more than one mind is better than a single teacher in a self contained classroom (See Green and Petty).

The Self Contained Room

The self contained classroom has been a standby for many years as a way of grouping pupils for instruction. Here, a single teacher teaches almost all curriculum areas. The self contained classroom may experience pull outs of pupils by the remedial reading instructor as well as the special education teacher for selected specific areas of instruction. For example, the remedial reading instructor may need to teach a pupil one on one in the area of reading. The special education teacher may have one or more main streamed pupils taught in a small group for specific periods of time. The self contained classroom, too, might have special music, art, and/or physical education teachers to teach in their respective areas of specialisation.

The self contained classroom has numerous advantages, over other plans of grouping for instruction, which include the following:

1. the teacher can get to know children well be teaching them for the majority of school time. This makes it possible for the self contained teacher to get to know each child well in terms of past achievement, as well as know each child

developmentally; an improved curriculum might well result when using this information to plan lessons and units of study.

2. the teacher may again use previous plans of lesson/unit construction, if these worked well and provided for individual differences. Some modifications will need to result due to summative evaluation of these plans. The teacher may make notes on these plans as to changes which need to be made.

3. the teacher can generally be more effective in parent/teacher conferences when knowing the offspring's parents more thoroughly due to having taught the same children during the school year.

4. the teacher might provide for different patterns of grouping for instruction within the self contained classroom. Thus, the teacher can emphasize teaching the class as a whole, small group/committee work, as well as individual endeavours of pupils when developing the curriculum. Highly flexible grouping plans may be used to encourage optimal learner achievement (See Burns and Schell).

Non-graded Schools

Pupils may be grouped in non-graded classrooms for the elementary school years. Thus starting with what is called, normally, the first grade level, pupils my be grouped homogeneously based on reading achievement. There has to be an adequate number of six year olds to group pupils homogeneously. Thus, if there were five roomfuls with 20 pupils per room, for example, a good chance would be there to secure a fairly homogeneous set of learners per room. The pupils in any room will always present differences in one way or another such as in reading, mathematics, science, and social studies, music, art, and physical education achievement. Interests, hobbies possessed, and motivation will provide for further differences.

With each roomful then of 20 pupils in homogeneous grouping, the teacher may further divide each roomful in terms of high, low, and average achievement in reading.

The teacher needs to place each child into the group he/she will do best in within the framework of homogeneous grouping. Fast achievers can complete more than one grade level in achievement in one school year. Thus, in the top roomful of the five given as examples, they may have completed second and third grade materials, and even beyond, at the end of the first year of schooling after kindergarten. Careful records need to be kept of each roomful of pupils as well as the subgroups therein. For the next school year, pupils begin with where they left off the previous school year. Thus, for example, if in the slowest achievement level of the five roomfuls of pupils, a subgroup is reading toward the middle of first grade reading materials, they would begin have at for the next school year. Pupils do not skip achievement levels nor do they advance beyond the level they can achieve in realistically, at the present time. Continuous progress from each pupil, regardless of the present reading level, is desired. Grade levels are merely mentioned to identify the past and present achievement level of the learner. Otherwise, there are not grade levels in the non-graded elementary school, but achievement levels are spoken of instead. With the example of five roomfuls of six year olds and three subgroups per classroom, can make for fifteen different reading levels. What is then emphasised in reading at the end of a school year provides a sequential beginning for the new school year (See Share).

Open Education

Open education procedures, as the name indicates, provides choices of opportunities to learn such as a learning centres approach in reading instruction. The teacher then needs to establish an adequate number of centres with each having enough tasks to make it possible for pupils individually to select what to read, as well as to omit what is not deemed to be purposeful. Each learning centre should have a clear title pertaining to the kinds of library books thereon. The following are examples:

1. nature, the zoo and circus, as well as farm animals.
2. people of other nations.
3. historical, geographical, among other academic disciplines.
4. classical books such as A Christmas Carol by Charles Dickens. These writings may be simplified including Classics Illustrated such as Tom Sawyer as well as Huckleberry Finn.
5. narrative content such as books by Dr. Suess.
6. encyclopedias from several publishers.
7. science library books including those on the changing surface of the earth, as well as library books on mathematics including the history of mathematics and the metric system.
8. different modes of transportation.
9. inventions in society.
10. space travel and missiles.

For each learning centre, a task card should list about five tasks for pupils to do to show comprehension. For example in centre number one, pupils may read a library book on nature. To indicate comprehension in reading about penguins, pupils might select a problem area such as how penguins can survive in the Antarctic. By going to the encyclopedia centre, the pupil may find needed information therein (See Wolfe)...

Open education may or may not have open spaces. Thus, learning centres psychology many stress having centres in the regular classroom as well as within open space architecture. Selected buildings which were built with open spaces have had walls built to separate the different classrooms. Open education must permit.

1. pupil choice in ascertaining what to learn, with teacher assistance when necessary.
2. pupils determining how to be evaluated after the completion of a task.
3. pupils sequencing their choices in terms of which library books to read.
4. pupils may also choose their very own library books when sustained silent reading is being emphasised (SSR).
5. pupils reading library books pertaining to a unit of study being taught such as on "volcanos" relating to a science unit on the *Changing Surface of the Earth.*

There can be pupil/teacher planning of learning centers or the teacher may develop the different centres with enough tasks so that pupils may omit doing those which do not possess perceived purpose. Each centre may be introduced by the teacher to secure learner interest and attention. Bulletin board displays may help to entire pupils having an inward desire to read selected library books. Not every library book can be introduced from the diverse centres, by any means. Each centre, however, should be introduced and a library book held up from that centre for all pupils to see. As the library book is held up the testier may mention in a sentence or two what the contents are related to (See Doll).

Departmentalisation

There are very few schools which have departmentalisation on the primary grade levels, except for music, art, and physical education. More schools emphasize departmentalisation on the intermediate grade levels. Here, there may be specially trained teachers, for example, to teach mathematics and science. Also, those teachers, not specially trained, who like and are very strong in science and mathematics instruction may then teach these academic areas while other intermediate grade teachers might take to teach social studies and the language arts instead. The arguments for departmentalisation of subject matter on the intermediate grade levels are the following:

1. subject matter is becoming increasingly complex to teach.
2. subject matter needs to be challenging for intermediate grade pupils and a well qualified teacher is needed to teach here, especially for gifted and talented pupils.
3. subject matter taught should be interesting to teachers. An enthusiastic teacher is needed for teaching intermediate grade pupils, as well as for all levels of instruction (See Victoria, 1993).

Teachers are then able to do advanced degree university course work in their chosen academic area of speciality. Integration of subject matter is still possible by planning together with other teachers who teach a different academic discipline.

In Closing

There are definite advantages for each plan of grouping pupils for instruction, as presented above. Thus:

1. basal textbooks have a manual to provide suggestions for instruction. The manual may be used flexibly and teachers may incorporate their very own ideas, also, for teaching and learning situations in assisting pupils to achieve optimally.
2. individualised reading, developmentally, is based on pupils choosing what they like to read.

3. multi-age grouping might assist pupils to learn to work together with younger as well as older individuals. People in society interact with others of diverse age levels.

4. transition rooms aide pupils to receive instruction which helps them to "catch up" with others in the same classroom.

5. team teaching emphasizes pupils working with the class as a whole, small groups, and individual endeavours. In society, people work on these three levels when interacting with others.

6. the self contained classroom provides a plethora of opportunities for the teacher to stress integration of subject matter.

7. the nongraded school emphasizes pupils achieving continuous progress which all should do, regardless of the kinds of going patterns which prevail.

8. open education stresses pupil achievement in decision making. Life itself consists of pupils making choices among alternatives.

9. departmentalisation stresses teachers teaching in their area of subject matter specialisation.

REFERENCES

1. Burns, Paul C., and Leo Schell (1973), Eds., *Elementary School Language Arts.* New York: Rand Mc Nally and Company, Part One.

2. Doll, Roand C. (1986), *Curriculum Improvement.* Boston: Allyn and Bacon, Inc.

3. Ediger, Marlow and D. Bhaskara Rao (2000), *Teaching Reading Successfully.* New Delhi, India: Discovery Publishing House, Chapter Twenty-two.

4. Ediger, Marlow, and D. Bhaskara Rao (2001), *Teaching Social Studies Successfully*. New Delhi, India: Discovery Publishing House, Chapter Six.
5. Ediger, Marlow (1988), *The Elementary Curriculum*. Kirksville, Missouri: Simpson Publishing Company, Chapter Eight.
6. Gordan, et. al. (1995) *"School Principals' Perceptions,"* Education, 116(1) 9-15).
7. Green, Harry and Walter Petty (1975), *Developing Language Skills in the Elementary School*. Boston: Allyn and Bacon.
8. Gunning, Thomas G. (2000), *Creating Literacy Instruction for All Children*. Boston: Allyn and Bacon, Chapter Eleven.
9. Lieu, Donald J. (2000), *"Exploring Literacy on the Internet,"* The Reading Teacher, 51(1), 63.
10. Moss, Barbara, and Judith Hendershot (2000), *"Exploring Sixth Graders Selection of Non-fiction Trade Books*, 6-17.
11. Shane, Harold, et al. (1962), *Improving Language Arts Instruction in the Elementary School*. Columbus, Ohio: New York: McGraw Hill Book Company.
12. Victoria, Palio (1993), *"The Arts and Psychology,"* Philippine Education Quarterly, 22(3), 20-28.
13. Wolfe, Don M. (1972), *Language Arts and Life's Patterns*. Second Edition. New York: The Odyssey Press.

Analyzing Student Difficulties in Reading

A Good reading teacher is able to analyze problems faced by students in reading and remediate that which is necessary. These are generally complex situations involved in reading instruction. Quality teachers:

1. are highly knowledge about methods and procedures of reading instruction.
2. take much interest in the welfare of learners in the school setting.
3. show they care for each student to become a proficient reader.
4. emphasize a child centered philosophy of teaching.
5. begin with where each student is presently in reading achievement and then work for optimal growth for each (Ediger and Rao, 2000, Chapter One).

Diagnosis and Remediation in World Identification

The reading teacher needs to be a good observer of student reading habits to notice where to intervene in order to improve skills and attitudes of the reader. Each student is unique in reading achievement and yet there are selected common errors made by learners in reading. First, the learner may not make adequate use of context clues. All students should be taught to use this skill in determining the correct word in contextual situations. Meaning theory is involved here. Thus if a student does not know a word in context, he/she should use the other words in the sentence to ascertain the unknown. Sometimes, more than one sentence may be read to identify the correct word.

If students provide outlandish guesses to replace the unknown word, the reading teacher needs to help the reader to provide a word which does make sense. Students tend to be aware of words that are not meaningful within a sentence. Sometimes, this is not adequate for a student to identify the correct word since several words provided may each be meaningful and yet not be the correct one.

Second, useful phonic elements need to be taught. An unknown word might begin with a familiar consonant letter. The consonant letter may then provide the key to the reader as to what the correct word is which fits into the rest of the sentence contextually. There are advocates of a strong phonics programme of sequential sounds/symbol relationships be taught. Intensive phonics for young readers will then be in the offing. The scope and sequence of the reading programme may then consist of phonics instruction largely with some time being given also to reading comprehension. The author takes the point of view that phonics should be taught as needed in context. Generally then, phonics would not be taught as isolated entities, but as needed to students within an ongoing reading lesson. Vital grapheme/phoneme relationships need to be in the repertoire of students. Diagnosis and remediation need to occur to assist students to become independent in word recognition techniques (Ediger, 1999, 15-18).

Third, if a student does not recognize a word while reading, he/she may be aided by noticing a prefix or suffix in the ongoing reading lesson. For example, the word "unusual" is not being identified by a learner, he/she might then be assisted by removing the "un" prefix. The student may have experienced the word "usual" and identified it correctly previously. The prefix "un," is very common in certain words. With the learner putting together two known, he/she is ready to proceed in reading meaningfully. The student should not spend an excessive amount of time in struggling to identify any unknown word. After attempting to identify a word for approximately five seconds, the student should be given help by using a diagnosis and remediation approach in order to become an independent, confident reader.

Fourth, students may lack background information needed to read the ongoing subject matter meaningfully. A major task of the reading teacher is to provide and discuss the necessary facts, concepts, and generalisations prior to reading a given selection. A variety of concrete, semi concrete, and abstract experiences presented in an understandable way eight well guide students in acquiring background information to attach meaning to what is being read. The background information relates directly to the ongoing reading lesson. It behooves the reading teacher to observe discussion settings to notice if students can relate the previously acquired knowledge with the new subject matter being assimilated.

Fifth, oral reading should be done with expression using voice inflection. The first of three ingredients of voice inflection is *stress*. Here, the reader pronounces a word louder than the others within a sentence. A monotone voice says all words orally on the same level of stress. With voice inflection, the reader interprets content read and pronounce words on different levels of stress depending upon the interpreted meaning when orally reading a given selection.

Linguists generally recognise four levels of stress from softness to loudness in oral language. A second ingredient of voice inflection is *pitch*. Pitch emphasizes words being said aloud pitched higher or lower, just as notes in a musical score are placed higher and lower on a staff. To interpret content spoken aloud, the reader needs to pitch selected words higher and others lower. A third ingredient of voice inflection is *juncture*. Here, the reader needs to pay careful attention to commas, periods, question marks, exclamation points, and quotation marks. It makes much difference in the meaning of a sentence if careful attention is not being paid to punctuation marks. For example, if a student omits all commas in reading the following sentence: At the picnic they had ham sandwiches jello salad and milk; how many food items were served at the picnic? It is difficult to say. It depends upon where the commas are placed to be read orally as pauses. There could be as many as five and as few as three food items at the picnic. It is important to interpret carefully in terms of what is being read aloud as well as silently. Diagnosis and remediation is salient in the use of voice inflection by students. Otherwise misinterpretations may readily come about.

Diagnosis and Remediation in Comprehension

Students should acquire not only vital facts from reading, but also more upward to more complex levels of thought. There is nothing at all wrong with reading and remembering factual information. After all, is moving upward on the scale of higher levels of thinking, facts provide the involved foundational learnings. Facts to be acquired should follow selected criteria including the following:

1. they are important in helping students to understand and ongoing selection.
2. they are vital and salient.
3. they aid learners to understand what will be stressed in higher levels of cognition.
4. they are useful now as well as in the future.

5. they cut across the curriculum and integrate well into many academic disciplines.

A second kind of information read has to do with understanding inherent subject matter being read. Reading for understanding aids in retention of subject matter. Thus, meaning theory is very important to stress in a quality reading programme. With meaning attached to what has been read, the learner can answer questions pertaining to content read in his/her very own words. This is different from answering questions covering subject matter read using textbook language or attempts to do so. Students should have maple opportunities to reflect upon what has been comprehended so that understanding and meaning might be emphasised within a group/collaborative setting.

With reflecting upon understandings acquired in a meaningful way, the student is perhaps entering into a higher realm of cognition such as using ideas in a utilitarian way, the third level of cognition. There should be ample opportunities in the reading curriculum for learners to use in new ways that which has been learned. With use made, the student is better able to retain ideas gleaned through reading. They like to perceive that content read can be used in practical as well as novel ways. Relevancy in the reading curriculum is an important concept to emphasize in ongoing lessons and units of study; critical thinking. The reading teacher needs to observe if each student is making application of previously learned subject matter in reading. This does need to be evaluated since a good reading curriculum emphasizes using quality assessment techniques to notice learner achievement and progress as well as to plan sequential lessons of instruction.

Fourth, the teacher must be an advocate of implement teaching strategies to aid students to analyze content read. To analyze means to divide what has been read into component parts. These component parts should include separating the factual from opinions, the fanciful from realness, and the useful from the non-useful, such as in seeking possible answers to questions. The detection of bias as well as jumping on the bandwagon are further areas for analyzing subject matter read. The reading teacher then has vital responsibilities to notice if students are inquiring into what has been read and not merely accepting content as being factual and possessing absolute truth.

Being gullible and naive certainly can be costly to any human being in school and in society (Ediger, 1976, 7).

Fifth, the reading teacher needs to guide students to engage in creative thinking involving that which has been read. To engaged in creative thought, the reader needs to develop original, unique ideas based on content acquired. Novel ideas are definitely wanted in creative thinking. In supervising student teachers in the public schools, the author has noticed that selected teachers have been highly successful with brain storming procedures. There generally are salient questions to ask learners over subject matter read. The question may involve many possibilities as answers. A plethora of possible answers from students may then be explored and printed on the chalkboard or typed with the use of an overhead projector. Each response must be treated respectfully with all students being encouraged to engage actively in generating ideas within the brain storming activity. Reading teachers need to asses if all are participating in a creative thinking atmosphere. As more and more ideas are being generated, it becomes increasingly difficult to add to those recorded responses without duplicating on previously presented ideas (See Ediger, 1978, 18).

Sixth, students do need to become proficient in the problem solving arena. Problem areas may be identified by the teacher and/or students from the ongoing reading selection. These problem areas require deliberation and intensive thinking. Once the problem has been clearly defined, information from a variety of reference sources may be used to secure needed information. The information acquired needs to be sorted out in terms of what is salient to solve the problem and what is reliable subject matter as compared to that which does not meet these criteria. A tentative hypothesis should result which is to be evaluated with further reading and study. The hypothesis is revised and modified, if need be.

Problem solving abilities are needed in almost all situations in life and are important skills to develop. The reading teacher needs to assess how well students are doing in each facet of problem solving. Diagnosis and remediation are important ingredients here (Ediger, 2000, 59-68).

Developing Good Attitudes Toward Reading

Selected students seemingly have quality feelings toward reading whereas others may tend to be more reluctant to read on their very own during spare time. What might a teacher do to assist students to do more reading? The following are offered as suggestions:

1. have a quiet reading corner in the classroom where students may read library books? A sign could be placed here to indicate the salience of reading library books at this place.
2. have a discussion centre whereby those students who wish to discuss a reading selection may do so with peers? The discussion may zero in on a multiple copy of a library book.
3. have enticing bulletin board display on recently purchased library books to what learner appetites to read?
4. have times devoted to introducing new library books briefly to students? Fascinating methods need to be used to encourage reading.

5. have a reading club for students to share library books read?
6. have a reading fair whereby students select their favourite book read in developing a related project to show at the fair?
7. have a bi-weekly newsletter sharing with parents what is being done in the classroom to encourage literacy endeavours among students?
8. have an author of children's literature come to school to discuss subject matter written?
9. have children attend a Children's Literature Festival at a nearby University?
10. have parents and grandparents come to the classroom on designated days to read aloud to students?
11. dramatize story content read?
12. video-tape an ongoing discussion in reading to indicate to learners in a positive manner what has been achieved and what is left to accomplish in being able to work well in a collaborative setting?
13. have students fill out a self evaluation form on what is liked as well as what is not liked in the literature curriculum?
14. have students in dyads change off reading a given selection orally to each other in a certain area of the classroom?
15. invite the school principal into the classroom to read orally to students?
16. devote time to Sustained Silent Reading—SSR. (Ediger, 2001, 79-83).

The reading teacher may evaluate each student's attitudes based on observations made during conferences using a five point Likert scale when responding to the following criteria: The student is:

1. reading an increased number of library books as indicated in conference settings.
2. improving in comprehension as indicated by comparisons made of notes made of previous to later conducted conferences.
3. making progress in using higher levels of cognition.
4. shows an inward desire to consume more literature appropriate for his/her present achievement level.
5. appraises the self when reflecting upon what has been read (Ediger, 1986-1987, 43-49).

Portfolios also should help students develop an increased interest in the world of literacy. Why? Students individually need to be actively involved in developing his/ her portfolio. They own the portfolio and their personal efforts are used, with teacher guidance, to develop the final product in ongoing self evaluation. What might a student then place into a portfolio to communicate achievement?

1. cassette recording in comparing earlier with later oral reading activities to indicate learner progress.
2. a videotape to show student achievement in committee work involving the discussion of a reading lesson.
3. drawings to reveal compression pertaining to the setting of story.
4. snapshots of a diorama made to make known the meaning of selected concepts read in a selection.
5. diagrams developed to indicate comprehension, such as in governmental organisations when reading across the curriculum.

6. a time line to show sequential labelled events in history.
7. written work on book reports, outlines, summaries, and conclusions.
8. journal writing on daily activities in reading.
9. a personal vocabulary chart, an experience chart, teacher written test results, diary entries on school work, as well as logs summarizing the diary entries.
10. puppets made and used to breathe life into a story read.

Products and processes placed into a portfolio provide excellent opportunities for diagnosis and remediation of learner difficulties in reading. For example in number one cited above, the student with teacher guidance may diagnose and then remedy *specific* problems faced by the learner in reading. Then too, the portfolio may provide information on the student's overall accomplishments in reading. Optimal achievement is an over riding end objective in reading instruction! (Ediger, 2000, 136-144).

Individual differences may be provided for by using Multiple Intelligence's Theory. Students may then use an individual intelligence possessed to reveal what has been learned such as doing an art project to indicate comprehension in reading (See Gardner, 1993). As a learning style, individual versus collaborative endeavours, is another factor which needs consideration when providing for each student in the reading curriculum.

REFERENCES

1. Ediger, Marlow (1978), "Write On,' *School and Community,* 65(2), 12.
2. Ediger, Marlow, and D. Bhaskara Rao (2000), *"Teaching Reading Successfully."* New Delhi, India: Discovery Publishing House, Chapter One.

3. Ediger, Marlow (1986-1987), "Reading Readiness and the Learner," *Minnesota English Journal*, 27(2), 43-49.
4. Ediger, Marlow (1976), "Objectives and Oral Communication," *California English*, 12(4), 7.
5. Ediger, Marlow (2001), "The School Principal: State Standards Versus Creativity," *The Journal of Instructional Psychology*, 28(2), 79-83.
6. Ediger, Marlow (1999), "Teaching Reading in the Social Studies," *Arizona Reading Journal*, 26(1), 15-18.
7. Ediger, Marlow (2000), "Peaking Activities and Reading," *Reading Improvement*, 37(3), 136-144.
8. Ediger, Marlow (2000), "Writing, The Pupil, and the Social Studies," *College Student Journal*, 34(1), 59-68.
9. Gardner, Howard (1993), *Multiple Intelligences: Theory Into Practice*, New York: Basic Books.
10. Searson, Robert, and Rita Dunn (2001), "The Learning Style Teaching Model," *Science and Children*, 38(5), 22-36.

Quality Discipline in the Classroom

The teacher who spends much time on disciplining pupils may find that instructional time is minimised and hindered. There needs to be a classroom which is conducive to teachers teaching and pupils learning. The noise level needs to be kept down to a point whereby pupils can learn and achieve optimally in each curriculum area. Time spent on discipling children is time taken away from achieving the objectives of instruction. The teacher in the classroom needs to have appropriate guidelines to use in teaching as well as specific workable procedures which help pupils to achieve.

Philosophy and Psychology of Classroom Discipline

Problem solving procedures emphasize teachers observing a contextual problem in disciplining pupils in an ongoing lesson or unit of study. The identified problem is clearly stated to that it can be solved. Information is gathered from a verity of reference sources and or from reflective thinking. The teacher then develops a tentative answer to the problem. The answer is an hypothesis, ready for evaluating in the classroom setting. Should the hypothesis not work, additional information and reflective thinking is involved with a new hypothesis forth coming.

Even a new problem may be developed along the way in problem solving procedures.

Problem solving procedures do not stress throwing the hands up in frustration, feeling that nothing can be done to minimize disruptions in the classroom. The problem solver stays with it and works on solutions until one is found.

Problem solving stresses the practical endeavours with in the school setting. Real and like situations are in the offing. Practical solutions are found to problematic situations. It is best if a set of teachers cooperatively identify and solve problems. However, a single teacher may also engage in problem solving philosophy and psychology. Sequential stages in problem solving are developed within the teacher, not decided upon externally. Teachers then intrinsically identify and solve problems. Consultant help and assistance may be asked for and used by involved teachers, as the need arises. Creativity is inherent since novel, unique solutions are needed to solve problems. The "tried" and "true" may not work in solving a problematic situation. Problem solving does not stress:

1. absolutes, but uses flexibility in the identification and solving of problems.
2. predetermined, ready made answers and solutions to problems, but rather personal initiative.
3. quick solutions to problems, but rather deliberation, thought, and perseverance.
4. hierarchical arrangements of individuals, but rather all can be involved in problem solving who are effected by the decision. Thus, a teacher may develop standards of conduct with pupils in a classroom and cooperatively enforce, in educationally sound ways, adherence to these standards.

5. intents of people involved in decision making, but rather the consequences of the act are viewed in the disciplinary arena, as well as in other areas of the curriculum (Dewey, 1916).

Behaviourism as a psychology of education may also be called realism in the philosophical arena. Behaviourism stresses predetermined measurably stated objectives in their use to develop an appropriate learning environment. The objectives pertaining to classroom discipline are determined by the teacher and printed clearly for all pupils to see and understand. The meaning of each measurably stated objective needs to be clarified and understood by learners. It is clear then to pupils if they have violated a standard. Either a pupil has/has not broken a rule. There is no guesswork involved.

Realists believe in the certainty of knowledge. Only what can be verified by others is true. True knowledge can be tested to see if it is upheld by others, using the same methods. Scientific methods are used to ascertain knowledge and skills. Attitudes of objectivity are needed. Supernaturalism does not exist since it goes beyond sense data. Objective thinking is inherent. The emotions and feelings of individuals are to be left out when securing information. Precision and accuracy are necessary when objectives are stated, implemented, and evaluated (Ediger and Rao, 2003, Chapter One).

Traynor (2002) identifies the following approaches used by teachers in school discipline:

1. coercive: A teacher using a coercive strategy to maintain order used intimidation and expressions of anger. This approach is characterised by the use of sarcasm, yelling, threatening, and demeaning students.

2. laissez faire: teacher tolerance of learner behaviour with pupils being permitted to govern their very

own behaviour individually. No external means are generally used to discipline pupil behaviour.

3. task orientated: the teacher tries to keep pupils busy with non-purposeful as well as purposeful learning activities.
4. authoritative: the teacher individually develops rules of conduct and strictly enforces them with no pupil involvement.
5. intrinsic methods of disciplining pupil behaviour whereby pupils learn to govern their own conduct (Traynor, 2002).

It is an ideal to guide pupils to govern themselves in the disciplinary arena. From within, the pupil then has standards which govern relationships between the self and others. To be this, problem solving would definitely by involved since the learner realizes that there are difficulties which need identification and solutions found.

Being Well Prepared for Teaching

Being well prepared for each day of teaching should help to curb discipline problems. It is salient to plan, for each lesson, those activities which engage the learner in the curriculum. Active involvement in learning opportunities helps to maintain learner attention in ongoing activities. Passive learners tend not to comprehend nor care for what is being taught. The objectives, the aligned learning activities, and appraisal procedures should all interrelate into a whole.

The following criteria should then be used by teachers in planning the curriculum:

1. the interests of pupils should be aroused so that learners pay careful attention to each ongoing lesson. If pupils lack interest in learning, the attention span might lack focus and encourage

behavioural problems. Disruptive behaviour is not helpful to both the teacher and pupils in a classroom. Pupils lose valuable instructional time due to inattentive behaviour. To learn as much as possible, pupils need to attend to that which is taught in order to attain objectives of instruction.

The use of voice inflection can do much to secure learner interest in the ensuing lesson. Thus proper intonation, stress, pitch, and juncture, as well as eye contact, should aide in obtaining learner attention to what is being presented.

2. the needs of each pupil must be met so that increased time is placed upon learning. These needs may include developing feelings of belonging to a group and as well as feeling accepted. To be an isolate must be painful due to a school setting being a social setting. Positive interaction with others and being accepted as one having worth is extremely important. Worrying about being called negative names must make for feelings of being uneasy and apprehensive. Needs of pupils may also emphasize meeting esteem goals. Thus, a pupil desires to be recognised for what can be achieved well. Pupils individually have their strengths and these need identification and use.

3. the purposes of pupils need to be increased so that reasons for learning are apparent. The teacher should assist pupils to perceive values in what is to be accomplished. A lack of purpose for learning makes it so that pupils are uncertain as to what has value to acquire. The purpose needs to be stated clearly by the teacher for pupils pursing objectives in each lesson. This may take a minute of time. An inductive procedure might also be

used. If the teacher has pupils speculate on what the purpose of a lesson is, then induction is involved and more time would be needed here, as compared to using deduction with the teacher stating reasons for the ongoing learning activity.

4. adequate background information needs to be a part of the pupil's repertoire so that the previous lesson is related directly to the new learning opportunities. If subject matter to be acquired is unrelated to what is known presently, the pupil may not be able to hurdle the gap between the new and the old learnings. It is well worth the teacher's time to make certain that each pupil has the prerequisites is order to benefit fully from the ensuing experiences.

5. meaningful subject matter and skills must be presented. With meaning, the pupil understands what is taught and can benefit from the instruction. If pupils do not understand what is taught, nonsense learnings might well be in evidence. To bridge the gap between previous content acquired and nonsense learning is not possible. The teacher or a knowledgeable peer needs to assist learners within large group, committee endeavours, as well as individually to attach meaning to what is being taught.

6. a variety of materials needs to be used in the teaching and learning area. Pupils differ from each other in terms of what kinds of instructional materials are most beneficial. Concrete (objects, realia, and items), semiconcrete (illustrations, video tapes, pictures, slides, filmstrips films, CD ROMS, the internet, among other pictorial forms), and the abstract (listening, speaking, reading, and writing activities) should be used as teaching

methods and materials to provide for individual differences among learners (See Fisher, et al., 2002).

7. learning styles of pupils need adequate attention in teaching and learning. Thus selected pupils work best together in a group setting whereas others do best in studying by the self. Flexible grouping patterns may be used to provide for different styles of pupil learning. Paying attention to the conditions of learning is time well spent. Each pupil's learnings should be optimised and teachers attending to styles of learning might well help (See, Searson and Dunn, 2001).

8. multiple intelligences need to be recognised and adequately provided for. Pupils differ from each other in terms of strengths possessed. Pupil A might like and be strong in mathematics and the ability to reason therein. Pupil B might have equivalent strengths in mathematics but achieve at a higher level in verbal skills such as in reading and writing. The two curriculum areas mentioned do interact with each other in that reading is required in both. In addition to reading word problems, pupils also need to learn to read mathematics symbols. In the area of writing, pupils do write across the curriculum, including mathematics. However, working with numeracy is the heart of the mathematics curriculum whereas literacy is the major goal of verbal intelligence. Thus, teachers do need to pay adequate attention to the intelligence(s) possessed by a pupil and develop these optimally (See Gardner, 1998).

9. quality sequence in learning must be provided for. The previously acquired learnings must seamlessly harmonize with the new content. From the pupil's perspective, he/she needs to experience a

psychological sequence whereby the learner, with teacher guidance, orders his/her very own experiences as in choosing sequential library books to read in individualised reading. A logical sequence emphasizes the teacher selecting the order of learning opportunities for pupils to pursue. The belief here is that the teacher, with his/her educational teacher training, is in the best position to select the order of activities for learners individually to pursue.

10. evaluation of achievement might well be done intrinsically such as the pupil with teacher guidance assessing the self in terms of desired criteria. Portfolios developed by the pupil with teacher help may also involve intrinsic procedures. Opposite would be extrinsic evaluation procedures such as state mandated testing, teacher written tests, standardised testing, and teacher observation.

A well planned series of lessons and units of study need to actively involve pupils individually, so that optimal learning is taking place. Pupils need to experience quality learning opportunities so that instructional time increases and discipline problems become less. Obtaining pupil attention is a key item in teaching and learning situations. Pupils who do not attend find time for day dreaming and entertaining others during instructional sessions. Thus, it is salient to establish *set* whereby a pupil pays attention to the beginning aspects of a lesson being taught (See Ratckin, et al., 1985).

Additional times also need to be given to establishing set other than at the beginning of a unit of study only. What is it that establishes set? This can be something which truly does obtain pupil attention, such as the following:

1. an enlarged illustration which all can see that indicates a key idea in a fascinating way. The

teacher might then have pupils brain storm what they see in the illustration. Each idea is to be respected and accepted. Pupils, individually, may even write what they see. Each item is numbered and there is no duplication of oral or written ideas. These kinds of activities involve all pupils in active learning. After the written brainstorming session, pupils in committees of four members may join together those concepts listed which overlap.

2. objects from a unique culture, relating directly to the unit taught, being displayed on a table or held up for all to see to captures pupil attention. Brainstorming again is possible as to how each object is used or starting which culture it came from, among other procedures. But, it also can be held up for all to see for a sequential, stimulating discussion. Unique objects can secure learner attention in a plethora of cases and situations.

3. learning activities with high pupil involvement should always be used. These include creative dramatics whereby learners use subject matter acquired to present a dramatisation. Parts to be played can be worked out and eventually all should have a chance to perform in dramatizing subject matter known in a creative way. It is fascinating for pupils to think of what fits in, for their individual part, when performing in front of a class. The play parts are not memorised but inherent subject matter is well known so that each participant can contribute in a meaningful manner. If desired, the play parts from a unit may be written out by committees of pupils. After which, it can be decided who plays which part. Volunteering for each play part can be salient. However, just so everyone has a chance to be in the play, it might be necessary for the teacher to appoint these oral contributions.

Reader's theater can also involve many pupils. In fact, there can be a set of pupils for each reader's theater presentation. As the name indicates, pupils individually read their own play parts containing the direct quotation only. The script is right in front of the participant for oral reading. Each pupil is seated in a chair for the reader's theater presentation. The part should be practiced and polished for high quality oral reading. The background information, for the individual direct quotation read, should have a separate reader who also has practiced the reading of the necessary ideas which provide structure for the direct quotes. The reader's theater, as well as the creative and formal dramatisations, may be performed in front of other classrooms of children. Receiving praise for doing well assists in developing the self concept of a learner. There might well be little time for misbehaviour with stimulating learning opportunities.

Specific Methods in Handling Discipline Problems

The involved philosophies and psychologies, as well as improving the curriculum, are all good means of helping to develop a quality programme of discipline. Then, too there are specific methods which may be used as methods to encourage good discipline.

- A time out area should be available where a pupil goes to, after violating one or more rules off conduct. The time out area needs to be removed from other pupils in the classroom. It could be an enclosed small area in a classroom. This gives the pupil a chance to reflect upon correcting his/her behaviour and then reentering the regular classroom for instructional purposes. The duration of time being in a time out area would be up to the teacher to decide and needs to be kept flexible. The pupil in the time out area may do school work or meditate upon what he/she would change. A time our area has helped pupils to redirect their behaviour in a positive direction.

Developing a plan to reenter the classroom may be made by the pupil who has broken the rule of conduct. The pupil needs to state, when asked by the teacher, what he/she did when breaking the/a rule. This must come from the offender only, and be given orally to the teacher. The plan must state what the pupil will do to correct the offensive act. The pupil must agree not to do the same negative behaviour when reentering the regular classroom. All rules of conduct are printed on a chart for all to see in the classroom.

- Positive reinforcement methods might be used. The late B. F. Skinner was a leading proponent of behaviourism Shankaranarayana (1990) wrote the following:

For Skinner (1969). "Teaching is an arrangement of contingencies of reinforcement which expedite learning." Skinner believes that promotion of learning is possible by giving attention to the following factors: the behaviour to be learned, the reinforcers that may be used, and the scheduling of reinforcers.

Skinner recommends the use of programmed instruction which provides for individual differences by allowing students to achieve at their own rate of speed. In terms of Skinner's Operant behaviourism, "a programme can be seen as an arrangement of material that will lead pupils to emit correct responses and will also provide reinforcement for that response ... the essential elements of programmed instruction ... are (1) an ordered sequence of stimuli, (2), specific student response, (3) immediate knowledge of results, (4) small steps, (5) minimum errors (6) gradual shaping of terminal behaviour.

According to Skinner then the most important task of the teacher is to arrange conditions under which desired learning can occur. Considering the fact that teachers are to bring about changes in extremely complex behaviour, they should be specialists in human behaviour. Effective and efficient manipulations of the multitude of variables affecting children's intellectual and social behaviours cannot be accomplished by trial and error alone, nor should such work be based solely on the personal experiences of the teacher, since this covers only a limited range of circumstances. Consequently, a scientific study of human behaviour is vital in the improvement of teaching because it provides accurate and reliable knowledge about learning and leads to the development of new instructional materials, methods, and techniques. Similarly, an empirical analysis of the teaching process is essential, for it clarifies the teacher's responsibility through a series of small and progressive approximations. This approach make teaching practices more specific, thereby facilitating a more effective evaluation (Morris and Pai, 1976).

Here, pupils individually or collective are rewarded for good behaviour. Tenets of behaviour modification are used in positive reinforcement. In other words, pupil are rewarded for exhibiting good behaviour. The standard or standards for pupils to achieve are announced ahead of time so that each learner knows what to do to receive the reinforcement. The following announcement(s) might then be made, as examples:

1. each pupil who receives a 95 per cent or higher of words spelled correctly from the weekly list may choose a prize from the reward centre. Small inexpensive prises might then be in the offing such as a pencil, a rabbit shaped erasure, a piece of candy, among others. The author when supervising university student teachers in the public schools noticed that even an attractive picture cut from a discarded magazine, can make a good reward which a learner may choose for doing well, such as in spelling.

2. a popcorn party will be held Friday, before school dismissal, for all who have not violated rules, as posted in the standards of conduct, located on the bulletin board.

Pupils need to be certain they understand what a rule violation means. The standard may be upped, and then needs to be announced prior to the holding of the popcorn party.

3. inexpensive teacher aide made badges may be given as rewards for doing well.

The teacher needs to be creative and think of what might reward a pupil for doing well in class. These can then be given to deserving pupils.

* Problem solving procedures might be used to encourage good behaviour. When a violation of a posted rule of conduct has occurred, the entire class might discuss possible solutions to the problem. The agreed upon solution may then be implemented. If the solution is inadequate, a new solution may be tried and implemented. A quality learning environment is necessary so that the teacher can teach well and pupils can learn in an optimal manner. Problem solving procedures take time, but have many inherent values. Thus, in school and in society, individuals alone or collectively, are always identifying and attempting to solve life like problems (Ediger and Rao, 2003, Chapter Eight).

REFERENCES

1. Billman, Linda Webb (2002), *"Aren't These Books for Kids?"*
2. Dewey, John (1916), *Democracy and Education.* New York: The MacMillan Company.
3. Ediger, Marlow, and D. Bhaskara Rao (2003), *Philosophy and Curriculum.* New Delhi, India: Discovery Publishing House, Chapter One.

4. Ediger, Marlow, and D. Bhaskara Rao (2003), *Elementary Curriculum*. New Delhi, India: Discovery Publishing House, Chapter Eight.
5. Gardner, Howard (1993), *Multiple Intelligences:* Theory Into Practice. New York: Basic Books.
6. Fisher, Douglas, et al., *"Seven Literacy Strategies Which work,"* Educational Leadership, 60 (3), 70-74.
7. Morris, Van Cleve, and Young Pai (1976), *Philosophy and the American School*. Boson: Houghton Mifflin Company, 340.
8. Shankaranarayana, B. L. (1990), *Achievement in Mathematics Under Guidance Discovery Learning and Reception Learning Conditions*. Ph. D. thesis Mysore, India, University of Mysore, 6, 7.
9. Ratckin, N., et al. (1985), *"Why Teachers Resist Content Reading Instruction,"* Journal of Reading, 28, 432-437.
10. Searson, Robert, and Rita Dunn (2001), *"The Learning Styles Teaching Model,"* Science and Children, 38 (5), 22-26.
11. Traynor, Patrick (2002), *"A Scientific Evaluation of five Different Strategies Teachers Use to Maintain Order,"* Education, 122(3), 493-510.

9

Societal Trends and the Curriculum

Teachers and school administrators need to be students of studying and analyzing trends in society. These trends need to provide content for studying objectives in curriculum development. The curriculum becomes increasingly relevant as it is based on what exists in society and what their implications are for pupil learning. There are a plethora of trends in society, but a few will be chosen to assist students of the curriculum to think of what is relevant to emphasize from the societal arena. Trends chosen may very from area to area, but no doubt, there will be commonalties.

The growing emphasis upon scripted teacher proof programmes and regimented student tasks has marginalised time for purposeful thinking and meaningful dialogue. This loss is significant because reflection supports students and teachers in connecting with what they already know, considering alternative perspectives, solving problems, and organizing their experiences for future use. The way we spend our time in schools and universities indicated what we value, and the loss of time to reflect indicates a shift away from valuing students and teachers as thinkers (Short, et al., 2002).

Which Trends Are Important?

The learning environment through the project approach can provide students with many attractive work choices and opportunities to develop interests in collaboration with their peers. In the this learning context, students are able to negotiate with the teacher to address their own personal learning needs and style preferences as well as curriculum outcomes. Research about effective learning from the fields of psychology and neuroscience continues to emphasize the importance of a addressing student interests (Chard and Flockhart, 2002).

Unemployment in a region appears to be a perennial problem. The problem may be that jobs are indeed scarce. There is futility in going to the unemployment office to seek listings of places to work. At the unemployment office, the lines might be long. Feelings of disgust may be there due to negative reports on job possibilities. The problem may be, too, that there are jobs, but they require much education and/or training. For example, the following may appear as job openings at the employment office:

1. diesel engine mechanic wanted.
2. trained carpet layer wanted.
3. cabinet builder wanted, work experience in this area necessary.
4. pharmacists wanted, previous experience desired.
5. veterinarian wanted in an established small animal hospital.

Numbers four and five of the above require much education such as the pharmacist as well as the veterinarian with a degree from an accredited university. Numbers two and three require highly developed skills learned over the years at the work place, such as in becoming a good carpet layer or cabinet builder. Number one above, being a diesel mechanic, requires meeting vocational and technical school requirements as well as quality practical experience.

Workers still may be able to obtain fast food restaurant jobs. These tend to pay minimum wage with no health insurance coverage and with no retirement plans from these companies being in the offing. Those who lack education and training for specific professions and prestigious jobs are left out of having the good things in society. Pertaining to these trends, what are the implications for pupils in the curriculum who presently are in the public school setting?

1. pupils need to achieve as optimally as possible in the school setting. Higher education or vocational technical schooling should be in the offing. A highly educated and trained work force needs to be in evidence so that increased knowledge, skills, and abilities are shown by workers to employers at the work place.

2. pupils need to assess personal strengths and weaknesses so that increased data is available for decision making in securing a future job or position (Ediger, 2002, 191-195).

Trend two emphasizes the importance of clean air and clean water. With a plethora of pesticides and herbicides being used to control animal pests as well as weeds, the federal, state, and local governments need to be vigilant about people using too many chemicals in the environment. To develop and maintain a clean environment, conducive to healthful living is a must. Without a quality physical environment with clean water, futile situations exist for human beings. It takes healthy human beings to think about and implement innovations necessary to project the environment. The following become important items in curriculum development pertaining to the natural environment:

1. an adequate number of units of study need to be developed and taught pertaining to "Living in a Clean Environment."

2. a careful selection of knowledge, skills, and attitudinal objectives should be emphasised in the curriculum. A variety of evaluation techniques need to be used to ascertain pupil present progress as well as determine what is left to teach.

3. a good current events curriculum might well keep pupils abreast of news about the environment (Parker, 2001).

Trend three stresses the importance of conserving energy sources. Automobiles, heavily used, do contribute to their share of energy use. Inefficient home use of energy sources also contributes to the heavy use of valuable natural resources. Fossil fuels are heavily used and cannot be recreated. Once the fossil fuels are used up, there are no additional fuels of this kind available. Thus, petroleum products are valuable and they are nonrenewable. It then becomes necessary to harness and use more of the renewable energy sources.

1. wind in which those who have installed generators to be propelled by wind find their home heating bills greatly reduced. In fact, a wind propelled generator can actually put more current into a power line as compared to what is taken therefrom. This amounts to income to be received by those who possess the wind driven sources of energy.

Two wind farm developments companies are after Wichita Country's wind resources, hoping to build 200 to 300 foot tall wind turbines on the western Kansas prairie.

It was Wichita Country's Economic Development that helped get Renewable Energy, Systems North America and enXco interested in the area's wind. A predominately agricultural community with 2500 residents, the organisation was looking for a way to boost the economy.

Both companies hope to do just that if the project is deemed feasible.

"Western kansas is the Saudi Arabia of wind," said Bud Pickle, project consultant with enXco... Of course, Kansas has wind everywhere."

About fifty people attended the wind farm discussion Thursday during the Wichita Country Economic Development meeting hoping to learn more about the proposed project (Bickle, November 23, 2002).

2. water whereby the sloping stream, oceans, or river sends currents at a high rate of speed which in return drives the commercial generator to produce electricity. Water, here, is renewable, but there are problems with pollution in that sea life has died due to overheated water coming from cooling the generator. Problems need identification and solutions are necessary.

3. geothermal energy which contains heat coming from the interior of the earth. It is expensive to tap this form of renewable energy so it can be used for heating buildings during the cold season. Reykjavik, the capital city of Iceland, uses much geothermal energy. The city of Monrovia, Utah also uses considerable geothermal energy.

4. solar energy is clean and a renewable source of energy. People who have houses with solar collectors have found that it can cut down much on costs of heating buildings. The power of solar energy can be noted when getting in to an automobile on a cold, sunny day. If the automobile has been parked in the open sunlight,

> the interior will be quite comfortable. It can be expensive to have solar collectors on houses, but it does save energy on heating buildings (See Holt Science and Technology, 2000, Chapter Six).

Nuclear energy has been used in certain places in the United States. Nearby Harrisburg, Pennsylvania is a large nuclear reactor which provides energy for this area of the United States. There is always fear of a breakdown of nuclear reactors, thus causing leakage of radio active products. It is extremely necessary to monitor radiation leaks which has caused harmful effects to individuals including cancer in its diverse forms. Pupils need to study different forms and sources of energy including coal and wood. They must learn about the concepts of renewable and nonrenewable energy sources. Also, it is salient to learn about the harmful side affects of using each energy source. With a spiraling number of human beings on the planet earth, it behooves all to conserve energy wherever possible. For example, it United States has grown from a population of 130 million in 1940 to 285 million in the year 2003. Each human being is a user of different energy forms. The question arises, "Can individuals continue to use energy to meet the increasing demands for sustenance and for a high life style?"

It is necessary to audit uses of different levels of energy. Thus, a building can become more economical in its use by turning off lights when these are not used. Better insulation of a building can make for tremendous improvements in the uses of energy. Turning the thermostat down to an approved temperature reading for night during the winter months can certainly make a difference in uses of energy. During the day time when school is in session, the thermostat should be set at a comfortable level, but not waste energy due to having an excessively warm classroom. Pupils need to study and help in monitoring ways of saving energy.

In an industrialised nation, there are always problems of what to do with solid waste products (See Guy, et al., 2002). Most of these are non-biodegradable such as car batteries, outworn refrigerators, ranges, dish washers, cars, tires, plastic pipes and toy, among others. Some of these items are recycled, in part, such as outworn car bodies. Biodegradable items do recycle such as weeds, straw, dead animals, dead trees, and crop residue. Hog complexes in which 100,000 hogs are raised and processed in one calendar year cause terrible odour problems. They also provide problems with what to do with the large amount of manure produced. Hog spills are somewhat common which contaminate the earth and can produce from ideal situations for disease. Even then, waste produce from hogs are recyclable. Can an industrialised nation keep manufacturing and continue to develop economically and yet maintain a clean environment? This will continue to be a major problem in society (See Preston and Herman, 1981).

Trend four emphasizes the importance of providing a good education for all. It is necessary to continue receiving as much formal as well as informal education as possible. One can never know too much about a given topic or field of endeavour. Standards keep going up in terms of educational needs of individuals. In the United States in 1940, for example, 50 per cent of the available students graduated from high school. Presently, the emphasis has been for all to graduate from high school as a minimal level. Estimates very as to how many do graduate. When the General Educational Development (GED) is included, the equivalent of 90 per cent end up as graduates. Is this adequate for today's sophisticated society? The answer is a resounding, "No." Post high school formal education should include a baccalaureate degree in a marketable area or vocational training for those so inclined. Vocational education, beyond high school, needs to have as much importance as does the baccalaureate degree from a university. There certainly is a real need for good automobile mechanics, builders of homes and other buildings, carpet layers, plumbers, and electricians. These are and must be highly skilled persons engaging in serving the practical needs of human beings in society.

Going beyond the baccalaureate degree emphasizes specialisation in diverse endeavours. Excellent teachers and instructors, school administrators, doctors, dentists, and lawyers, among other are certainly needed in society. The demands from each of these continually goes upward. People in society expect much, for example, from a medical doctor in today's society. The life span of individuals continues to rise. It is common to see newspaper obituaries of the deceased who have lived ninety years. At the turn of the twentieth century, the average age of death of individuals was fifty years; this has gone up to 74 years presently. Improved nutrition and better medical care has certainly increased the life span of human beings in the United States.

Pupils in the elementary school need to have an adequate number of units of study on healthful living and proper medical care. The well being of each person is important for optimal achievement being possible in the world of work.

Trend five stresses the wise use of leisure time. With a forty hour work week, people need to be able to use leisure time which enriches the self. Too frequently, individuals engage in doing things detrimental to personal health and a misuse of time. Immoral acts, drinking alcoholic beverages, tobacco use, and wasteful spending of money, takes its toll of individuals who should use their very own resources to read, travel, interact with others, engage in wholesome recreation, and participate in worthwhile clubs and organisations. Individuals also need to be involved in civic and community endeavours, working for the betterment of all in society.

Pupils need to experience quality objectives pertaining to the world of work as well as toward wise use of leisure time. Units of instruction taught on carefully selected careers, kindergarten through grade twelve, need to be chosen and put into operation within teaching and learning situations.

Trend six emphasizes the importance of health care coverage for people. Good health has become a privilege and not a right of citizens. People with high incomes can afford the best of medial care through insurance coverage. The low income persons probably depend upon good luck and thereby hope to a avoid illnesses requiring medical care, including hospitalisation. Poor people have medicaid as their provider of medical services, but this is, by no means, a substitute for medicare. Medicare, as well as medicate, is financed federally by the social security funds, coming from worker payroll taxes. To be sure to do well in school work and in life in general, all need to be covered with adequate health insurance. Good health care should be a right for all, not merely a privilege for the few. There are too many pupils coming to school who have disabling allergies, asthma, severe colds, and breathing problems from enlarged adenoids and tonsils. Eye glasses are needed by pupils who have defective vision. Added to these problems are mentally retarded pupils, individuals with Down Syndrome, hearing deficits, juvenile diabetes, autism, physically handicapped, and behaviourally disordered, among other handicaps. An increased number of Fetal Alcohol Syndrome children are also located in the school setting. It behooves all to be concerned about the rights of children, as well as others, in the societal arena. A society benefits as its individuals are able to live the good life. When a segment of society is permitted to fall through the cracks, then the totality of individuals realizes negative consequences, such as with crime in its many manifestations. The individual should not be separated from the group, nor should the group be separated from the individual, due to a community consisting of the whole, not a part of something (See Ellis and Esler, 2001).

Trend seven consists of a changing society. One thing is certain in life and that is the concept of *change.* Change is all around us. As one segment of society, there have been tremendous changes in agriculture.

The pupils should study how work is performed differently as compared to earlier times. Changes in manufacturing, at the work place, in the home, and at diverse places of business need to be studied, analysed, and understood. Pupils should develop attitudes of acceptance toward positive changes in the societal arenas. The school curriculum, too, needs to change as innovations appear on the horizon. Each innovation must be assessed in terms of inherent qualities. Blindly accepting what is new is not acceptable, but needs to be evaluated in terms of desired criteria.

Trend number eight stresses democracy as a way of life and as a form of government. Pupils in school need to learn about democracy as a major tenet being important in society. In the classroom setting, pupils with teacher assistance need to have opportunities to establish standards of conduct. These standards need to be reasonable, realistic, and realised. Standards such as the following are important in school committee work (Ediger and Rao, 2003, Chapter Eleven):

- all participate in the discussion and ongoing group work
- no one should dominate the deliberations
- careful attention should be given by participants to what transpires in committee endeavours
- respect for all participants is highly salient
- each person's ideas need to be respected

- esteem needs must be met whereby contributions from each are valued
- all should feel a sense of belonging to the committee or group
- rude behaviour needs to be identified and remedied. No one is an island into themselves
- each needs to contribute optimally; no one should let others do all/most of the work
- ideas need to be presented to the total group, not to a segment of members
- content and skills not understood should be clarified as to meaning and understanding
- higher levels of cognition should be stressed such as critical and creative thinking, as well as problem solving
- chair persons should invite all to participate, not just the few only
- self discipline is an ideal to strive toward for all committee members
- the interests of all committee members should be obtained
- discussions for purposeful committee work must be in the offing.

Committee endeavours need to be evaluated by participants with teacher guidance. The following need careful assessment:

- each pupil contributing to his/her optimum in committee work
- pupils working on meaningful projects until completion
- pupils respecting contributions of others

* pupils aiding each other to do their best in committee work
* pupils being interested in and perceiving reasons for leaning
* pupil products and processes being evaluated in terms of positive criteria
* pupils putting forth optimal effort to do the best possible
* pupils doing better individually than previously
* pupil interests being encouraged throughout the project toward completion
* pupils, individually, doing their best work possible, according to his/her abilities.

The area of motivation is both broad and complex. What seems to be motivating to one person is not to another. However, one often useful technique is to show learners what they will be able to do when they finish the instruction. This is more than a statement of the objective of the instruction, which is the next component of the instructional strategy. It is the instructor's demonstration, written description, or illustration of what the learner will be able to do. The initial part of the instruction may also consist of some historical background or interesting fact about what is to be learned. It is important to note that there is no objective for this information, so it will not be tested. It is simply a means of attracting the student to the instruction (Dick and Carey, 1985).

In Conclusion

There are a plethora of trends in society. The author has just scratched the surface of listing and analyzing these trends. No doubt, the following are equally salient:

1. wars and rumours of wars and the necessity of working out solutions, hopefully, between and

among nations involved are musts! The destruction of buildings, killing and maiming of human beings, developed mental illness of war participants, refugees, as well as bitterness and futility of life in losing homes and family members among others.

2. excess number of individuals in penal institutions, especially from minority groups. There is Inadequate attention paid to economic, educational, social, and individual successes of minority people

REFERENCES

1. Bickle, Amy (November 23, 2002), *"Two Companies Hope to Build Wind Farms in Wichita Country,"* The Hutchinson (Kansas, News, A-3.
2. Chard, Sylvia, and Marilyan E. Flockhart (2002), *"Learning in the Park,"* Educational Leadership, 60 (3), 56.
3. Dick, Walter, and Lou Carey (1985), *The Systematic Design of Instruction.* Glenview, Illinois: Scott Foresman and Company, 136.
4. Ellis, Elizabeth Gaynor, and Anthony Esler (2001) *World History:* Connections to Today. Upper Saddle River, New Jersey: Prentice Hall, Chapter Twenty-seven.
5. Ediger, Marlow (2002), *"Reading for Enjoyment and Pleasure,"* Experiments in Education, published by the SITU Council of Educational Research, in India.
6. Ediger, Marlow, and D. Bhaskara Rao (2003), *Philosophy and Curriculum.* New Delhi, India, Chapter Eleven.
7. Guy, et al. (2002), "Phase into Learning," *Science and Children,* 40 (3), 27.
8. Holt Science and Technology (2000), *Earth Science. New York:* Holt, Rinehart and Winston, Chapter Six.
9. Parker, Walter C. (2001), *Social Studies in Elementary Education.* Upper Saddle River, New Jersey: Prentice-Hall, Inc., Chapter Six.

10. Physical Science (1999), *New York: Glencoe...* Mc Graw Hill, Chapter Seven.
11. Preston, Ralph C., and Wayne Herman, Jr. (1982), *"Our Environment,"* Teaching Social Studies in the Elementary School, Fifth Edition. New York: Holt, Rinehart and Winston, Chapter Eleven.
12. Short, Kathy G., et al. (2002), *"Thoughts from the Editors,"* Language Arts, 80 (2), 91.

Curricular Issues in the School Setting

Issues in the curriculum need identification and indepth study. It takes time and effort to study each issues. Adequate resources need to be made available to read about and analyze each issue. Faculty members need time to study issues and discuss points of view taken. It is only through a discussion that a synthesis may be possible within an issue. It will not always be possible to arrive at a synthesis pertaining to each issue. Sometimes, a philosophical difference occurs and different school of through will be inherent in tackling an issue. There is a challenge involved in studying issues. Critical thinking is involved in that an issue needs to be sorted out in terms of pros and cons, resulting ultimately in putting the parts together to make a whole.

Curricular Issues in Reading

Continuous debate·exists pertaining to the teaching of phonics versus the whole language approach. This debate has consolidated into an either or situation, not a both/and philosophy of reading instruction. There are strong arguments which may be made for either position. First, the arguments for phonics instruction will be discussed. The English language is considered to be quite consistent between symbol and sound, according to phonics advocates. Thus, it behooves the teacher to teach phonics to primary grade pupils, in particular. A strong phonics approach in teaching emphasizes a systematic procedure. Thus, an entire K- 3 textbook may well provide techniques for teaching phonics to pupils systematically. The scope is clearly defined as to what will be emphasised. Sequence in pupil phonic learning will also be clear. Pupils then are to master diverse sound/symbol relationships. By learning to decode, pupils are increasing their individual strengths in learning to read. A letter or set of unknown letters might then be decoded in reading. First, pupils then need to learn to break the English language code and then read for meaning. Another procedure is to stress phonics and reading subject matter simultaneously in early childhood reading. Thus, increased meaning is stressed in the ongoing reading programme (Gunning, 2000).

Toward the other end of the continuum, whole language reading advocates believe that ideas come first, rather than phonics. With meaningful subject matter read, pupils will be more interested in reading as compared to learning phonics in initial reading experiences. One whole language approach in learning to read is the Big Book approach. Here, the teacher chooses an appealing book, appropriate for young children, whereby the content is large enough for all to see clearly in the instructional group. The teacher, first of all, assists pupils to develop background information for reading the ensuing lesson from the Big Book. Next, the teacher reads aloud the content and points to each sequential world while reading. Pupils follow along by looking at the words on the printed page, pointed to by the teacher, in the Big Book.

Next, the teacher together with pupils read aloud the identified words sequentially as the teacher continues to point to each word read. The story may be reread as often as desired or as needed. Pupils do like to hear stories reread. Pupils then are able to master world pronunciation within a story or context and yet hear ideas being read. Words are then recognised in context. With repeated reading, the pupil may learn to identify selected words not mastered from the first reading (See Clay, 1985).

A teacher might teach phonics, in degrees, when using the Big Book method of instruction. A gamelike atmosphere could even be present. For example if a word in the story read began with a "b" letter, pupils could be challenged to find other words beginning with a "b" letter/ sound. Or a rhyming word in the text might be located in the text pertaining to the word provided by the teacher. According to Fisher, et al. (2002), there are seven literacy strategies that work:

1. our literacy plan advises that teachers read to their students every day in every class for at least five minutes. Some teachers read the text aloud while students listen; other teachers read the text aloud while students read along. Most often, the selections are not from the textbook. Instead teachers select the materials that build student's background knowledge, provide them with interesting vocabulary words and ensure they are becoming fluent in reading...
2. ask students what they *know* about the topic to be read followed by the question, "What do you still *want* to learn?" A third question is, "What did you *learn* about the topic?" This procedure is designated with the letters ... KWL.
3. use graphic organizers to provide students with visual information which complements the class discussion or text.
4. assist students with vocabulary development.
5. help students in relating reading and writing by having students write related content to clarify ideas.

6. guide students to do structured note taking over content read.
7. implement reciprocal teaching methods.

Curricular Issues in Mathematics

There are issues which continually arise in each curriculum area, such as "getting back to the basics." It almost appears as if educators then have gotten away from the basics for some unidentified reason. The basics have never been clearly defined. Perhaps, what is a basic for one person may not be so for others.

In mathematics, some want to emphasize basic skills such as memorizing and mastering basic computations skills, while others advocate instruction that builds student's understanding of mathematical concepts before working on basic skills. The letter approach has been advocated by the National Council Teachers of Mathematics, which set off the current debate in 1989 when it published its standards for K- 12 math education.

While the initiative has yet to be publicly announced, the Education Department has already made a $4000,000 grant to three leaders of the basic skills movement for efforts to raise teachers' content knowledge—one of the major goals of the administration's (President Bush) approach. The recipients of the grant leads in the "back to basics" push in California, and these awards have led others in the field to maintain that the new initiative will have a distinct bias (Hoff, 2002).

What constitutes the basics in mathematics? The author will give his opinion on what might include the basics in mathematics. First, there will be much attention paid to scope and sequence of mathematics content for pupil mastery from the adopted basal textbook. The adopted textbook needs to view mathematics instruction as pupils becoming highly proficient in addition, subtraction, multiplication, and division. In addition to drill and practice on these four fundamental operations on number, word problems might also commonly incorporate the basic addition, subtraction, multiplication, and division facts. With word problems, pupils have opportunities to use the four basic operations on number in context. Dyads may practice these basics with the use of flash cards. One of the two pupils, here, may hold up the sequential cards for the other learner to respond to. The roles of the two pupils may then be reversed. Games might also be developed whereby three or four pupils may take turns lifting a face down card and answer what is thereon such as 4 + 3 = . If he/she answers correctly, the pupil moves forward one space on the game board. The next pupil lifts a face down card and also responds to the number pair it contains such as 7 + 2 = . The first pupil to complete the spaces on the game board wins the game. What ever is being studied in arithmetic may become items to list on the face down flash card such as 9 x 9 = . Thus, there are a variety of learning opportunities to stress in emphasizing the basics in addition, subtraction, multiplication, and division (Ediger and Rao, 2003, Chapter Eight).

With a proper grounding in the basics, advocates say, pupils may well become increasingly proficient in number use in algebra, geometry, calculus, and trigonometry. Proper sequence is needed for the pupil to move from the simple to the increasingly more complex in the mathematics curriculum. Advocates of the basics stress the following:

1. there is *essential* subject matter for all to master in mathematics.
2. the essentials or basics in mathematics need careful identification.
3. the basics need to be taught without the frills and fads of what is not essential.
4. pupils need to attend carefully to the learning opportunities presented.

5. distractions need to be avoided. The distractions include misbehaviour of pupils and frivolous learnings unrelated to pupils learning basic subject matter.
6. much drill and practice is necessary to master the basics.
7. pupils need to persevere in ongoing learnings pertaining to the essentials in mathematics.
8. developing interest in learning the basics is recommended, but not at the expense of learning vital mathematics content.
9. self discipline is necessary in order for each pupil to master the basics in mathematics.
10. the teacher, alone, is in charge of determining and implementing the basics curriculum. Carefully chosen textbooks, workbooks, work sheets, soft ware, and teacher made materials, may be used to implement the basics mathematics curriculum. Teacher made materials such as games must focus only upon essential learnings not trivia (See Rays, et al. 1995).

The basics might well stress a no nonsense curriculum whereby pupils acquire important, essential subject matter, not the fanciful nor the novel. Mathematics is an exact science whereby there is perfect agreement upon correct answers to computation and formulas. It is not based upon opinions, but rather upon fact. Philosophies have been developed by prominent philosophers in order to obtain preciseness in knowledge. Descartes believed that exact knowledge could be acquired by using the mathematical model in coming up with conclusions. He then advocated the use of clear and distinct ideas in the pursuit of knowledge. Thus, a person would begin the pursuit of knowledge with a general statement. Deductively, the individual would move forward as sequentially as possible in the pursuit of exact knowledge. When the individual is no longer able to move forward deductively, then that wold result in a clear and distinct idea, Early in his life time, Descartes was concerned about obtaining accurate knowledge, not opinions nor vague generalisations.

A second mathematician, Bertrand Russell, believed that all subject matter be stated specifically so that accurate communication among individuals is possible. He even advocated that there should be perfect agreement among words used in society. Astronomy would provide a model whereby each word used in communication has a corresponding concrete object. Thus to measure if an expressed idea is true, the correspondence theory needs to be used. A word used in communication must have its related concrete object (Russell, 1972).

Measurement of pupil achievement in mathematics needs to be precise with standardised testing instruments. Each pupil then in taking a test would have the same directions announced, the same allotted time for test taking, the same answer sheet used to assess pupil test results, and all other conditions being kept the same. With machine scoring of tests, human error in scoring should be greatly minimised, although computers do experience glitches!

Toward the other end of the continuum, the National Council Teachers of Mathematics (1989) emphasizes an inductive approach be used in teaching and learning situations. Induction stresses pupils moving from specifics to a generalisation in ongoing lessons and units of study. Thus, for example, pupils may be asked how many degrees the temperature dropped if yesterday the reading was 65 degrees and today's is 37 degrees. A new process then needs to be learned by pupils with regrouping and renaming. Pupils may then speculate on how to determine the number of degrees the temperature dropped: 65-37= . Each pupil may provide educated guesses on how to perform the operation in arriving at a correct solution. Committees may also be formed to come up with a correct answer. Inductive learning here also stresses problem solving whereby thought and deliberation are needed. With inductive learning and problem solving, the teacher guides the discussion but does not tell what the correct answer is or how to do the problem. Rather, the teacher provides minimal clues and cues for pupils to use in arriving at a correct solution.

Inductive learning and problem solving emphasizes the following:

1. deliberation and thought by pupils in problem solving, and not having fixed answers to questions.
2. use of read life like problems to have pupils ponder over, not a sole textbook approach in teaching mathematics. Word problems in basal texts do contain content for indepth learning for pupils and might well relate very closely to the real world of number.
3. learnings are paced according to what pupils can understand and attach relevant meanings to. Learners reveal the rate or pacing of subject matter content when they respond, meaningfully, to questions raised by the teacher.
4. responses to questions come from pupils, not factual content presented by the teacher.
5. pupils learn vital concepts and generalisations, not isolated facts.
6. predicting how to do a problem is in evidence, not fixed means of arriving at answers to problems.
7. pupil problem solving is stressed rather than memorizing facts.

8. flexibility in critical and creative thinking are in evidence, rather than rote methods, formal procedures, and rigidity of performing operations on number.

9. use of a variety of materials in teaching mathematics, not a basal textbook only.

10. varying procedures of grouping pupils for instruction such as having large groups, committees, and individual pupil endeavours, rather than teaching the class a whole only (See Peressini, 1997).

Pupils need to become mathematics literate in a rapidly changing world. The National Council Teachers of Mathematics (NCTM) in 1989 came out with a comprehensive statement of objectives for pupils to achieve. Five broadly stated objectives listed by NCTM are the following; Pupils need to.

1. learn to value mathematics.

2. become confident in their ability to do mathematics.

3. become mathematical problem solvers.

4. learn to communicate mathematically.

5. learn to reason mathematically (NCTM, 1989).

The above named objectives are indeed worthy for pupil achievement. If pupils value mathematics, they will believe it is a highly important area in the curriculum. Being confident in the self should also assist pupils to achieve at a higher level than would otherwise be the case. Pupils being good problem solvers is a major goal in teaching mathematics and is salient in society and in the future. Problem solving will always be important in the lives of individuals. Communicating well with others is practical and being able to communicate mathematical ideas in diverse ways is essential since individuals live in an economic world whereby goods and services are purchased/sold continuously. Quality reasoning is necessary in mathematics as well as in every day life's situations.

Concepts and generalisations to be acquired by pupils need to (be)

1. important now as well as in the future.
2. assist pupils to use knowledge in school and in society.
3. relevant in the minds of learners.
4. emphasize structural ideas in mathematics.
5. selected carefully by teachers, supervisors, and administrators.
6. implemented as objectives sequentially so that each pupil may achieve as much as possible.
7. taught as background information which might then be used by pupils in ensuing lessons.
8. balanced in terms of objectives for pupils to achieve knowledge, skills and attitudes.
9. integrated with subject matter from other academic disciplines as needed to provide a meaningful mathematics curriculum.
10. presented in an interesting manner to capture pupil attention for learning that which is important (Ediger and Rao, 2000, 55).

Quality guidelines are always important for teachers to consider and use in order to provide the best mathematical experiences possible for pupils.

Curricular Issues in Teaching Science

A strong science curriculum is needed to provide experiences for pupils to live in a world of science. The content and methods of science are equally salient. Objectives need to be chosen carefully including knowledge (vital facts, concepts, and generalisations), skills (performing experiments and demonstrations, critical and creative thinking as well as problem solving, and assessing the self in terms of desired criteria), and attitudes (wanting to learn more science, doing objective thinking, as well as desiring to work harmoniously with others).

Learning opportunities to achieve objectives should be varied to provide for individual differences. A developmental science curriculum is a must. However, needs of learners should be ascertained with appropriate attempts implemented to meet those identified. The chosen learning opportunities need to attract learner attention. They need to be adapted to the learner to provide for the talented and gifted, for average achievers, as well as for slow learners. Each pupil should achieve as much as possible. Thus learning opportunities should:

1. be motivational to provide energy for pupil's achieving challenging objectives.
2. be interesting to capture learner attention.
3. be purposeful so that each pupil perceives reasons for learning.
4. be meaningful so that pupils' attach meaning to important facts, concepts, and generalisations.
5. be designed to provide for individual differences.
6. be emphasised to incorporate knowledge pertaining to diverse styles of learning.
7. be adapted to provide for diverse intelligences.
8. be challenging and yet achievable.
9. be intrinsically rewarding.
10. be open to pupil's questions and comments (See Shaughnessy, 1998).

Too frequently, science has been a course stressing abstract learnings only. Rather, pupils should have ample opportunities to learn science through inquiry methods. Inquiry methods stress pupils learning by discovery. For example, in learning about the concept of "air takes up space" in an ongoing unit of study, each pupil in a committee may be given a small plastic sack. All objects, beforehand, must be put within the desk or away from the pupils' reach. Pupils individually then are to hold the plastic sack and put something therein. A pupil might then attempt to put a pencil in the sack, but the pencil is to be left in the enclosed desk. Finally, a pupil may move the bag through the air rapidly and yet hold onto it. The bag is now closed and learners may see that air does take up space. What transpired should be open to questioning and elaboration in an atmosphere of freedom and respect.

Experiments such as these involve pupils directly in a hands on approach to learning. Pupils make discoveries and these can be discussed in a stimulating manner with those involved. There can be deliberation, thought, and challenge in discovering knowledge and skills. Sometimes, the teacher may need to demonstrate an experiment to insure safety to pupils.

Adequate commercial science equipment needs to be available and the finger tips of participants. Science equipment might also be made in school within an ongoing unit of study, as well as learners and the teacher should bringing items from home for science experiments as they relate to what is being studied. Experiments and demonstrations then should be the heart of the science curriculum (See Blough and Schwartz, 1984).

Life like experiences for pupils abound which provide content for science learnings. A public school in which the author supervised student teachers had an adjacent nature trail. Here, pupils viewed with teacher guidance evergreens (non-deciduous trees) and deciduous trees (oak, walnut, poplar), in noticing likenesses and difference, especially in fall when the leaves of deciduous trees change colour. There were a few squirrels and rabbits, scampering among the trees, making for variety during the excursion. Careful observation is a trait of a scientist. Pupils also need to become good observers. They raised many questions during and after the excursion which require knowledge of the natural world. To answer questions, pupils used science encyclopedias, the basal textbook, the internet, CD ROMS, and video tapes, among other reference sources to obtain needed information.

A resource person from a nearby university might be invited to the classroom to answer questions which required specialised knowledge. Pupils may write journal entries about their school science experiences. These entries provide time for reflection and thought. Reflection by the learner over what has been learned should assist the pupil to retain previous learnings and develop salient generalisations. Important concepts learned then become an inherent part of each generalisation. A good kind of homework could involve a pupil interviewing an individual who has expertise in a given field of knowledge. The knowledge to be obtained may involve content discussed in an ongoing unit of study in science. Or, it might involve a personal area of interest such as the role of photosynthesis in plant growth. Field work can also be an interesting scientific endeavour for a pupil. One learner was excited about inspecting and studying different kinds of weeds in the home garden. These weeds, in season, included dandelions, sunflowers, ragweed, and foxtail. The learner carefully observed each part of the weed such as the roots, stem, and flowers of the dandelion. He read encyclopedia entries on weeds such as how the dandelion plants reproduce and spread their seeds.

Selected science teachers have stressed a seminar approach in learning. Here, the teacher assists pupils within a committee to choose a topic for indepth discussion. The committee does research in securing needed information. The purpose of the seminar is to guide pupils to thoroughly seek knowledge and intensify understandings. If pupils are studying a science unit on "Animals with Backbones," they may make indepth comparisons, for example, among fish, amphibians, and reptiles. In the seminar, these comparisons may be analysed, contrasted, and synthesized. Respect for the thinking of others is important in a seminar. Participants need to stay on the topic; the seminar needs to be open to questions and comments of involved pupils. Each participant needs to feel free to participate full to achieve optimally. A summary of the seminar needs to be available to participants. Continuous evaluation of the seminar needs to be in the offing to notice if pupils

1. are achieving ideas indepth.
2. are participating fully.
3. are attaining salient concepts and generalisation in the seminar.
4. are accepting of the ideas of others.
5. are realizing higher levels of cognition.

Pupils on their way to and from school may bring items of importance to the science unit being discussed in class. For example, a child might notice a sidewalk becoming uneven due to roots of trees uplifting portions of the walk. A good discussion and research on causes of these happening should be in the offing. Why are there rapid growth of roots from trees which damage an out door sidewalk? Rapid changes noticed, by one or more pupils in temperature readings, may also provide content for discussion in the classroom setting. Curiosity on the part of pupils needs to be fostered and encouraged. There is much science which pupils can learn on an individual basis.

A good current events curriculum can assist pupils to learn important science happenings. There are news items about floods, tornados, hurricanes, ice and snow storms, mud slides, avalanches, earthquakes, and drouth which capture pupils attention for discussion, elaboration, analyses, and synthesis. In fact, a good science current events curriculum might well parallel quality offerings in the ongoing science lessons and units of study.

A project method might be a good way for pupils to use a hands on procedure to achieve objectives in science. Here, pupils with teacher guidance need to perceive reasons or a purpose for doing a project. Pupils individually or in a committee then need to make plans to achieve the objective(s). The plans are carried out to fruition. Resulting projects require careful planning and carrying out of these plans. Ultimately, quality criteria need to be developed to assess the strengths of the projects. In a science unit on "Weather and How it Affects Us," the author has noticed while supervising university student teachers in the public schools, the following completed projects:

1. a wind vane, an anemometer, a rain gauge, and a barometer.
2. drawings of cumulous, cirrus, and stratus clouds with a major researched generalisation attached to each kind of cloud.
3. model sheet and gully erosion scenes.
4. a model solar collector.

Project methods permit pupils to use a hands on approach in learning. These projects may, not only be displayed in the classroom, but also visitors might be invited from other classroom in the school building.

A science fair may be planned and implemented in the school setting. Each participant then needs to develop a project to exhibit at the fair. A plan needs to accompany the exhibit with the following inherent items:

1. objectives for the project to achieve.
2. a brief description of how the project was made.
3. a statement of how the project will be used.

Clearly started criteria need development to judge the worth of each project. The following criteria, among others, might be used to assess each project:

1. neatness and completeness.
2. effort in its making.
3. usefulness.
4. positive attitudes toward working on the project.
5. an attitude of wanting to do additional projects.

Problem solving in the science curriculum is very important. Here, the teacher needs to guide pupils to identify a problem in context. The problem needs adequate delimitation so that it can be solved. Thus a delimitated problem such as the following may be asked by one or more pupils: "Why can a star fish acquire a new limb once one has been chewed off" Pupils in a small committees of three to four members might peruse references of diverse kinds to obtain necessary information. The information gathered needs to be organised in a meaningful manner in order to shed light upon the problem area. It takes time to organize and summarize information acquired from a variety of reference sources. Information needs to be analysed to separate reliable from unreliable data.

The issue then deals with using a hands on approach in learning about the natural world on the part of pupils versus traditional abstract learnings, only, stressed in a outdated science curriculum.

Issues in Teaching Social Studies

The social studies curriculum has revealed a plethora of changes which were made in the last two decades.

Instead of emphasizing history and geography, largely, social studies today stresses more social science disciplines. History is still an important discipline studied by pupils within the social studies, but there needs to be balance among the other social science disciplines when studying human beings. Studying human beings from a historical point of view, only or largely, is not adequate. History, in the social studies, too, has a different emphasis now as compared to earlier times.

The National Council for the Social Studies (1994) lists ten thematic themes to be included in a quality social studies curriculum. These are culture; time, continuity, and change; people, places, and environments; individual development and identity; individuals, groups, and institutions; power, authority, and governance; production, distribution, and consumption; science, technology, and society; global connections; and civic ideals and practices. The author will discuss history, geography, political science, economics, and anthropology/sociology as they relate to the teaching of social studies.

1. The teaching of history should stress time as it relates to changes in the human experience. With time lines developed by pupils with teacher guidance, learners might then clearly see the many changes which have occurred in society with the elapse of time. Comparing the time of the interstate and the very heavy traffic thereon with the very beginning of the automobile 100 years ago is truly a revolution! For example, the modern automobilies of today with heaters, air conditioners, and computerised parts has made for heavy use of service stations, restaurants, hotels/motels, and car repair services. The entire landscape has changed then with the introduction of the automobile. Changes do occur rapidly and will continue to do so.

Pupils need to accept change as a way of life. Change can make for multiple improvements in society, but it also has its harmful side effects such as pollution in its diverse forms.

2. Geography in the social studies needs to stress the concepts of place, region, interaction of places and regions, and change as revealed in land forms over the centuries. Pupils need to possess excellent knowledge and skills as to why regions differ from area to area and from different perspectives of latitude and longitude. Agricultural crops grown, industries possessed, natural resources in evidence, as well as use made of these resources must be known by pupils.

3. Political science, as a social science discipline, is an important discipline for pupils understand fully in the social studies. The concept of power is salient throughout the study of political science within the social studies. Different levels of government have power to govern and rule. The federal government with its legislative, executive and judicial branches exert much influence over the lives of people governed. State government has its laws, rules, and regulations which affect human beings. The kind of government in evidence will depend much upon the degree of freedom possessed by individuals. How friendly the government is to human beings in meeting needs and what is done to take care of disasters of different kinds affecting human beings may truly make or break a society. The free enterprise system or socialism have pros and cons, but their effect depends upon how the worth of each person is viewed.

4. Economics is an area which truly does affect human beings since all buy goods and services. Production is a key concept in that people are

producers and consumers of these goods and services. Within the status of a developed technological framework, people have definite wants and needs. How these are fulfilled differ from individual to individual depending upon available resources and the amount necessary to live a fulfilled life style. Labour, capital, land, and management are involved in the production arena. The level of technology possessed is an important consideration in a nation as to the kind of prosperity desired and developed. The quality of the labour force in terms of education and skills possessed make considerable difference as to how productive a society is. Opportunities for education can make for success in life, if ample, or a lack of success if low in intensity (See also Parker, 2001).

Issues in the Anthropology/Sociology Curriculum

A major emphasis of both anthropology and sociology is the study of culture. Culture stresses the human made part of society, as compared to the natural environment as studied by scientists. Thus, for example, pupils need to study the following about a nation, such as Jordan and the West Bank:

1. the language(s) of that country. Perhaps, a few words would be adequate for pupils to learn in Arabic to notice how a dialect of Arabic differs from the English language.

2. foods eaten such as rice dishes. Machluba, as a rice dish, contains rice, with chicken, as well as pieces of broccoli, egg plant, kousa, and cabbage. A native person from the Arab world or one who is very familiar with foods eaten in that part of the world needs to be invited to prepare a truly native food dish for pupils.

3. kinds of clothing worn, such as bedouin men wearing cloaks instead of coats, sandals instead of shoes, baggy pants instead of trousers, head dresses instead of caps/hats. Many dress in western wear in Jordan and the West Bank.

4. types of homes lived in. For example Bedouins live in moveable tents, instead of modern houses that other use as dwelling places. Bedouins keep interior items of a home to a minimum due to movement to better grazing lands necessary for their livestock. Thus, they tend to sit on the ground for relaxation and eating. The hands are used for eating rather than knives, forks, and spoons. Many people in Jordan and the West Bank do eat and relax using western kinds of furnishings and utensils.

5. villagers have permanent dwellings and grow olive trees, citrus fruits, vegetables (carrots, tomatoes, cauliflower, among others).

6. urban dwellers such as in Amman, Irbid, Jerash, Ma'lan, and Aqaba, increasingly dress in western style clothing. The Moslem religion is practiced by most Arabs, although 15 per cent are of the Christian religion.

7. tourism is a major source of income in times of relative peace. Places which tourists visit on the West Bank and in Jordan are the walled city of east Jerusalem, the Church of the Holy Sepulcher, built in 1142 AD; the Dome of the Rock, an octagonal Moslem Mosque built in 691 AD; the Mosque el Aqsa built in 712 Ad; The Western Wall, a remnant of the Ancient Jewish temple, built 2000 years ago; a Roman Amphitheater, built in the early days of the Roman Empire and located in Amman; two excellent castles—Kerak

and Shobeck—on the east bank of the Jordan River from the days of the Crusades (1099-1187 AD), and a mosaic map located in Medaba from the days of the Byzantine Empire (approximately 600 AD). Pupils need to view current travel brochures on the Holy Land and prepare an imaginary tour of that area of the world. Slides are available on the previously named sites. If a different unit in social studies is being stressed than on the Middle East named above. pupils may study people using the same categories listed such as the language spoken, clothing worn, foods eaten, types of homes lived in, agricultural crops grows, tourism, and/or means of earning a living. Also, a study of farming and manufacturing are salient to emphasize.

8. much of the Arab world. Recordings may be purchased or ordered from a music store. It would be good to have a native from the Arab world play several selections of music.

9. slides of archaeological findings of the Middle East may be discussed with pupils. There are slides available on archaeology of the Middle East from large photography stores. These need to have an accompanying guide which the teacher may use in teaching pupils. If the local school is close to a university with a department of archaeology, a professional may be contacted to see if he/she would come to talk to pupils using actual objects form a dig or illustrations showing the work of archaeologists (Ediger and Rao, 2001, Chapter Fourteen).

As pedagogy, multicultural education acknowledges the aims of social studies education to provide students with a foundation in history and other social sciences, and the skills needed to become critical decision makers. Its content for instruction is derived from a pluralistic society and membership in a global community.

Thoughtful patriotism is promoted in many ways in social studies to encourage students to be proud of their country and work to improve their opportunities and the world community. To play out these roles, citizens must possess self knowledge and knowledge of their immediate environments and beyond.

A multicultural framework in a k—12 social studies programme rests on this country's motto, E Plurabus Unum. its objectives are to develop student's critical understanding of ways in which diversity has both contributed to society's common civic ideals and values and to student's critical understanding of ways in which diversity has both contributed to society's common civic ideals and values and to students' sense of responsibility at addressing issues of democracy, equality, and social justice (Zong, et al., 2002).

REFERENCES

1. Blough, Glenn, and Julius Schwartz (1984. *Elementary School Science and How to Teach It.* New York: Holt, Rinehart and Winston.
2. Clay, M. M. (1985), *The Early Detection of Reading Difficulties,* 3rd Edition. Auckland, New Zealand: Heinemann.
3. Ediger, Marlow, and D. Bhaskara Rao (2000), *Teaching Mathematics Successfully.* New Delhi, India: Discovery Publishing House, 55.
4. Ediger, Marlow, and D. Bhaskara Rao (2003), *Elementary Curriculum.* New Delhi, India: Discovery Publishing House, Chapter Eight.
5. Ediger, Marlow, and D. Bhaskara Rao (2001), *Teaching Social Studies Successfully.* New Delhi, India: Discovery Publishing House, Chapter Fourteen.
6. Fisher, Douglas, et al. (2002), *"Seven Literacy Strategy Which Work,"* Educational Leadership, 60 (3), 70- 74.

7. Gunning, Thomas (2000), *Creating Literacy for all Children.* Needham Heights, Massachusett: Allyn and Bacon.
8. Hoff, David J. (November 20, 2002), "*Math Instruction, Like Reading,* Has Ideological Differences," Education Week, pages 19 and 24.
9. National Council Teachers of Mathematics (1989), *Curriculum and Evaluation Standards for School Mathematics.* Reston, Virginia: NCTM, 23.
10. National Council for the Social Studies (NCSS, 1994), *Curriculum Standards for Social Studies.* Washington, DC: NCSS.
11. Parker, Walter C. (2001), *Social Studies in Elementary Education,* Eleventh Edition. Upper Saddle River, New Jersey: Prentice - Hall, Inc.
12. Peressini, Dominic (1997), "*Parental Reform of Mathematics Education,*" The Mathematics Teacher, 97 (6), 426.
13. Reys, et al. (1985), *Activity Cards for Helping Children Learn Mathematics.* Boston: Allyn and Bacon.
14. Russell, Bertrand (1972), *A History of Western Philosophy.* New York: A Touchstone Book.
15. Shaughnessy, Michael (1998), "*An Interview with Dunn About Learning Styles*" The Clearing House, 71 (3), 145.
16. Zong, Guichun, et al. (2002), "*Multicultural Education in Social Studies,*" Social Education, 66 (7), 447.

Design in the Science Curriculum

Science teachers and supervisors need to be able to design a quality curriculum of science learnings for pupils. Science throughout the public school years needs to be taught well so that the lay public can truly see how important this curriculum area is for pupils. Too frequently science is left out of state mandated testing. Science teaching might then be minimised. Efforts in school go into preparing pupils for testing well in reading and mathematics as basics in the curriculum.

1. people live in a world of science. Happenings in the universe such as earthquakes, mudslides, tornados, hurricanes, cyclones, floods, lightening, avalanches, and snow storms, do occur rather frequently and can leave much havoc. There are enough of destructive natural occurrences whereby a daily current events programme from these events in science is possible. Pupils do need to understand possible causes for each and realize how the affects can be minimised, such as in properly constructed buildings to withstand earthquakes and tornados.
2. science, inventions, and technology have certainly made life more pleasant for human beings.

Centralised heating, air conditioning, grain elevators in farming to elevate farm crops to needed heights in storage bins, hydraulic lifts to load heavy machines from the floor level to where they are needed on truck beds, grain drills and plows among other farm machines attached to the tractor which may be lifted out of the ground with the pull of a lever, mash and water for laying hens automatically supplied to adjacent feed/water troughs, and the list goes on.

3. better health care is available and selected harmful diseases have been eliminated basically. The author has observed during his lifetime when polio badly crippled people for life and caused many deaths. Polio was frightening to parents, children, and the lay public as late as the 1940s. Presently, few people worry about polio. Drs. Sabin and Salk have truly been heroes with eliminating the threat of polio in society. Tuberculosis, mumps, whooping cough, among others, are seemingly a thing of the past. Medical science continues to move forward and needs to eliminate/minimize cancer, the common cold, rheumatism, heart attacks, strokes, among other leading diseases (See Ediger, 1984, 5-14).

These are just a few salient contributions made by the world of science. Science in the school setting needs to have its fair share of time devoted to its contents.

Trends in the Science Curriculum

Each school system needs to give careful attention to identifying and implementing relevant trends in the science curriculum. The study of vital trends should be ongoing. A professional library for teachers and principals should be available in the school library. Recent university level texts for teaching science should also be in the offing.

Professional education journals pertaining to science should be readily available to all in science education. These include *Science and Children,* and *The Science Teacher,* monthly publications from The National Science Teachers Association (1997). Teachers and school administrators should take time to read and study current literature in science. Visits should be made to classrooms of outstanding science teachers to observe exemplary instruction. Professional meetings need to be attended which stress science education. Workshops and faculty meetings for teachers and administrators need to devote time in stressing excellence in the science curriculum. Teachers and administrators should take university courses in improving the science curriculum. Online course work is definitely possible; however, an adequate amount of time in these courses should be a hands on approach in science learnings. Hands on science is the heart of the curriculum. Inservice education then needs to be available to participants to improve pupil teaching and learning in science.

In addition to studying/implementing relevant trends in teaching, teachers and school administrators also need to implement problem solving skills in science. For example, from current events discussed and science experiments conducted, curious pupils identify questions and problems. These need to be respected and encouraged. Problems, for example, which may be identified include the following, depending upon the science unit taught:

1. what causes an earthquake?
2. what might be done to minimize the chances of getting the common cold?
3. what uses can be made of magnets in society?

Once problems have been identified, information needs to be gathered for possible answers. A variety of sources need to be used which should result in an hypothesis—a tentative answer. The hypothesis needs to be evaluated in a practical situation. If the evaluations prove the hypothesis faulty, more information might be gathered or a new hypothesis developed and tested.

Third, experiments are at the heart of the science curriculum. Experimentation is done by scientists in a laboratory setting. Pupils should emulate the conducting of experiments. Each science unit of study should emphasize the setting up and doing of experiments. For example, in units pertaining to soil erosion, there are excellent experiments which may be performed. Thus, two boxes with the same amount of soil in each might be used. One has a grass covering whereas the other does not. Both boxes should have the same slant of about 30 degrees. The same amount of water should be poured on each. Pupils may then catch the run off in a jar and measure which has the greatest amount of erosion. The experiment must be carefully conducted so that one variable is measured only, and that being the amount of run off due to one box of soil having a grass covering. The results need to be measured and recorded. Accuracy is very important in measuring and recording. A hands on approach must be used in these experiments with active pupil involvement.

Fourth, pupils with teacher guidance need to use a variety of reference sources in problem solving and also to verify the outcomes of an experiment. Thus, science equipment, basal science texts, library books, video tapes, CD ROMS, slides, films, filmstrips, single concept film loops, among others, may be used in ongoing units to provide for individual differences among learners.

Fifth, a quality evaluation programme needs to be in the offing. Teacher observation using appropriate criteria, teacher written tests, pupil self evaluation, as well as state mandated test should provide data on what pupils have learned and what is left to learn. Diagnosis and remediation needs to be emphasised. Testing and evaluation should be used as teaching devices and stress what is left for pupils to learn. Testing and evaluation should be valid and cover that which has been taught. Content validity is usually to be in evidence. Reliability is equally important in that pupil results should be consistent be it test/retest, alternative forms, split half.

Sixth, an integrated curriculum has much merit. Knowledge which is related should be remembered better that which is in isolation. Seemingly, ideas which are related are remembered better due to sequential content being able to trigger off new ideas. If ideas are perceived in isolation, the human mind compartmentalizes and fragments content. Thus, the science curriculum may be integrated with the social studies in units pertaining to the environment due to social and natural forces being involved. If for example, there is drilling for petroleum in the Arctic region, a preserved natural area, then human beings are involved in drilling for pertroleum. Mathematics might well be the language of science and therefore the two academic areas tend to be integrated. The language arts areas of reading, writing, listening, and oral communication are and must be integrated throughout the science curriculum.

Seventh, quality sequence must be in the offing in science teaching and learning situations. Sequence pertains to *when* learnings are to be stressed. In order, when should science experiments be presented? Should they be presented first, second, third, or fourth in ongoing units of study? Good sequence or order is needed so that a previous learning may provide background information for the new learning to be presented (Ediger, 1999, 112-117).

Eighth, the scope of the curriculum needs to be flexibly developed to indicate planning of ongoing lessons and units of study. The scope should not repeat what had been covered in previous school years, but rather indicates an orderly progression of science units of study. Scope pertains to breadth of content to be covered. Should the breadth of subject matter to be covered deal with the earth sciences, the life sciences, and physical sciences largely or only? The breadth may be broadened to include the social sciences of geography, economics, and anthropology. It might also include music and art. Thus the scope may be broadened or narrowed from what it is now. Perhaps the earth sciences, the life sciences, and physical sciences would be broad enough in scope. Beyond that the question arises in terms of how much integration of content there is to be from other academic disciplines (Ediger, 2001, 120-123).

Ninth, Inquiry learning must be in the offing in the science curriculum. Here, pupils are involved in a questioning approach in learning science. Science is not taught through memorizing facts but through inductive methods. Inquiry processes emphasize observing phenomenon, hypothesizing pertaining to identified problem areas, experimenting, recording, generalizing, and communicating the results. (Ediger, 2001, ERIC, ED454274).

Tenth, individual differences among pupils need to be provided for. There are handicapped pupils who need accommodations in learning, gifted and talented learners who need to be challenged, and average achievers, who need to learn as much science as possible.

Objectives in Science Instruction

Objectives for pupils to achieve are a vital part of science curriculum design. These objectives need to be relevant and significant. A study of trends in the science curriculum help to determine objectives for pupil attainment. Three categories of objectives should result. Knowledge objectives stress important concepts, and generalisations pupils are to achieve. Careful consideration needs to be given to this category since knowledge does abound and yet that which is important needs to be taught. For example, in a unit tilted, "Stars in the Universe," the following relevant objectives may be identified:

- the apparent motion of stars each night is due to the turning of the earth.
- the apparent brightness of a star depends on its distance from the earth, its size, and its temperature.
- the milky way is one of thousands of galaxies that form the universe.
- the use of instruments has been very important in the study of astronomy.
- the solar system is a tiny speak in the vast Milky Way.
- distances in the universe are measured in light years.
- everything in the universe is in motion.
- our sun is a star.
- constellations are patterns of stars (Blough and Schwartz, 1984).

These become knowledge objectives of instruction for pupils to achieve in ongoing lessons and units of study.

A second category of objectives are *skills* ends. Skills objectives indicate that pupils use the knowledge obtained in viable ways. The following are provided as examples of skills which are valuable for pupil attainment:

1. being a good observer. The learner does not jump to hasty conclusions in a science experiment, but observes carefully what actually does transpire.
2. identifying questions and problems. In context or as the need arises, the pupil identifies gaps in knowledge which require necessary information.
3. communicating ideas clearly. In a discussion setting, the learner presents ideas orally that

possess meaning and clarity. Being able to communicate effectively is a must in studying scientific phenomenon.

4. measuring accurately in the scientific world is important. Science tends to stress numerical data, such as in measuring force, distance, velocity, acceleration, average speed, among others, in the physical sciences.

5. classifying knowledge to bring order and meaning from a mass amount of information. Thus, vertebrates may be classified in terms of fish, amphibians, reptiles, birds, and mammals.

6. achieving reliable inferences. Not always is knowledge and data presented in a clear cut manner with precision, thus requiring pupils to make inferences. For example, in reading United States population figures covering the years 1890-2000 from a table in terms of ten years intervals, a pupil needs to inter what has transpired in trends and in time. Reading between the lines is necessary here.

7. thinking scientifically. Here, the pupil needs to be objective and remove all biases in thinking. Wherever the truth may lead in scientific investigations, the pupil is willing to follow evidence and analyze information.

8. using reliable information sources. These include quality experiments and demonstrations, objective conclusions reached by qualified individuals and groups, reputable textbooks, science encyclopedias, significant internet and world wide web sources of scientific information, CD ROMS, trade books, video tapes, films, filmstrips, illustrations, drawings, diagrams, excursions, as well as concrete, semiconcrete, and abstract materials of instruction, in general.

9. being open minded. In science pupils need to invite verifiable facts, concepts, and generalisations for discussions in problem solving. Testing ideas in problem solving, as well as using experiments and demonstrations, are salient in the science curriculum. Opposite of openness is the closed indoctrinated mind which does not accept evidence, even though it is trustworthy. Appreciating the methods of science in obtaining trustworthy information is vital for all children.

10. thinking critically by separating facts from opinions and accurate from inaccurate ideas. Creative thinking is also vital in bringing about new, novel ideas. Originality of thought is truly an instigator of progress and achievement. Each ideas needs to be appraised and assessed to come up with the best thinking possible (Ediger and Rao, 2001, Chapter Two).

A third category of objectives, namely attitudes, are equally salient as compared to knowledge and skills ends. Attitudinal objectives emphasize feelings which individuals possess or should develop. Attitudes assist or might hinder pupils from achieving. The following are worthwhile objectives for pupil development in science:

1. being curious pertaining to the natural environment. Curiosity does make for increased learning on the part of pupils. The inward desire to learn is truly important.

2. being a responsible learner to fulfil tasks, promises, and responsibilities.

3. showing traits of perserverance. This pupil is not one who gives up easily in pursuing a task.

4. doing the best work possible under existing situations.

5. assisting others as needed in ongoing lessons and units of study (Ediger, 1995, 14-15).

Learning Opportunities to Achieve Objectives

The objectives are that which the teacher uses as benchmarks for which pupils should strive. Learning opportunities provide impetus for pupils to achieve acceptable objectives of instruction. *Initiating activities* set the stage for pupils in learning about a new science unit of study. The following are appropriate ways to motivate pupils in having an inward desire to learn from the new science unit:

1. a bulletin broad display with a caption and neatly arranged illustrations which draw pupil attention to the new unit of study.
2. a science experiment or demonstration which captures pupil curiosity.
3. a nearby excursion whereby pupils see how science phenomenon studied in class can be related to the natural environment.
4. a video tape which presents information and illustrations on what will be stressed in the ongoing unit of study.
5. a resource person presenting content on his/her area of speciality while relating it to major objectives of instruction.

Initiating activities have important facets to stress in that they are to provide adequate background information to pupils in order to benefit from the new unit in science. They also are to arouse pupil interest for the ensuing unit of study. The previous unit studied by pupils should then lead seamlessly into the new unit in science.

Developmental activities assist pupils to achieve the stated objectives of unit instruction. They stress indepth teaching, not survey approaches. Each pupil needs to achieve as optimally as possible. Pupils here need guidance to recall salient information. They need to understand that which was recalled. Merely recalling facts is of little value unless they are understood by pupils. It is always good to apply and use what has been learned. Analyzing what was used indicates a higher level of cognitive objective. Analyzing pertains to breaking the subject matter acquired into component parts for assessing. Then, synthesizing content needs to come into being. With synthesizing, the pupil puts back together the relevant parts of what was analysed. Finally, the worth of the synthesised content needs to be determined (See Bloom, 1956).

Culminating Activities. Here, pupils are emphasizing the closing of the unit being pursued. There needs to be a relevant summarizing of subject matter learned. Otherwise, there will be a hodge podge of unrelated accrued ideas, difficult to remember. Pupils also have opportunities to review and rehearse previous learnings in the culminating activities pursued. A structure or framework of salient generalisations achieved should result during the culminating activities. The kinds of activities which assist pupils to draw conclusions should be in vogue. These activities include reading, writing, project methods, dramatic experiences, experimentation and demonstrations, construction activities, oral communication, listening activities, discussions, reports, and collaborations among peer work, among others. Computer technology should be used adequately be it in software packages, word processing, and data storing from resulting experiments and demonstrations. Individual differences need to be provided for so that each pupil may achieve optimally (See National Science Teachers Association, 1997).

Evaluation of Pupil Achievement

There are numerous evaluation techniques to ascertain pupil achievement in science. Common techniques which have been used in designing and determining pupil achievement include the following:

1. multiple choice and true/false.
2. completion and short answer.
3. matching and essay.
4. self appraisal in terms of desired criteria.
5. rating scales and checklists.
6. anecdotal statements.

More recent procedures of assessment include

1. journal writing by the teacher and also by the pupil.
2. video taping teaching and then assessing the contents therein by using proper standards.
3. state mandated testing with the use of either criterion referenced tests (CRT) or standardised tests (norm referenced tests).
4. rubric use and simulation teaching. According to Freiberg's research (2002), pertaining to a low-inference self assessment measure in a simulated lesson taught by a first year teacher in a week long summer academy, the latter determined that she needed to:
    - allow more wait time for students to respond to higher level questions.
    - ask a question, leave time, and then call on a student.
    - allow more student questions and feddback.
    - narrow the topic.
    - fully review previous concepts and tie this new lesson in with previous lessons.

- use more specific praise.
- stop saying OK and all right.
- do this self assessment more often to examine and assess progress.

REFERENCES

1. Bloom, Benjamin S. (1956), Editor, *Texonomy of Educational Objectives*, Handbook One: Cognitive Domain, New York: David McKay Co., Inc.
2. Blough Glenn O, and Julius Schwartz (1984), *Elementary School Science and How to Teach it*. Seventh Edition. New York: CBS College Publishing, p. 199.
3. Ediger, Marlow (2001), *"Reading Science Content"*. Hoosier Science Teacher, 26 (4), 120-123.
4. Ediger, Marlow (2001), *"Assessing Inquiry Learning in Science,"* ERIC, ED454274.
5. Ediger, Marlow, and D. Bhaskara Rao (2001), *Teaching Science Successfully*. New Delhi, India: Discovery Publishing House, Chapter Two.
6. Ediger, Marlow, and Digumarti Bhaskara Rao (2003), *Teaching Science in Elementary Schools*. New Delhi, India: Discovery Publishing House.
7. Ediger, Marlow (1984), *"The Psychology of Learning,"* Journal of Education and Psychology, 42(1-2) 5-14.
8. Ediger, Marlow (1999), *"Problems in Teaching Science,"* Experiments in Education, 27(7), 112-117.
9. Ediger, Marlow (1995), *"Designing Science Units of Study,"* School Science, 33(1), 14-15.
10. Freiberg, H. Jerome (2002), *"Essential Skills for Teachers,"* Education Leadership, 59(6), p. 59.
11. National Science Teachers Association (1997), *National Science Educational Standards*. Arlington, Virgini: NSTA.

Quality in the Social Studies Curriculum

The social studies needs to the designed carefully and with much thought and deliberation so that the best curriculum possible is implemented for pupils. Within the social studies, pupils need to understand their past (history), the regions which affect them (geography), the political institutions which govern (political science), the economic institutions which provide needed goods and services (economics), the institutions which provide structure and influence in society (sociology), and culture (anthropology). These six social science disciplines provide core knowledge for the learner in ongoing units of study in the social studies. One of three categories of objectives for pupils to achieve are *knowledge* ends; here, the six social science areas provide subject matter for learner achievement. Pupils though instruction may then achieve vital facts, concepts, and generalisations (Ediger and Rao, 2002, 6-11).

Objectives of Instruction

Selected knowledge objectives which pupils may achieve in each social science discipline and emphasised in unit teaching are the following:

History. The pupil will select a present day news happening and provide three events which lead up to the selected occurrence.

Geography. The pupil will describe the region where each of the above named events occurred, while using a map and a globe.

Political science. The pupil will compare and contrast the system of government being stressed within the region being studied with a different form of government in a removed area.

Economics. The pupil will survey the goods and services developed and exchanged within each region.

Sociology. The pupil will study, reflect upon, and indicate how religious institutions affect human behaviour.

Enthropology. The pupil will state how culture (language, customs, attire, music, art, foods eaten, and types of homes, among other items) affect human behaviour (Parker, 2001).

Knowledge objectives provide subject matter for pupils to achieve. Subject matter, here needs to be relevant and developmental for pupil attainment. Objectives need to be challenging and yet attainable. Worthwhile objectives can come from social scientists, the teacher, and learners. The latter contribute objectives when they raise questions in class for reflection and for problem solving.

A second category of objectives emphasizes *skills* ends. Skills stress the importance of pupils using and applying subject matter (knowledge) acquired in ongoing social studies units of study. Uses and applications may include the following:

Analyzing. Here, the pupil separates facts from opinions, fantasy from reality, accurate from inaccurate statements, as well as detects band wagon approaches, and political correctness.

Creative thinking. This might well involve putting ideas together after taking out the unimportant and irrelevant as in analyzing. Novel and unique ideas also are salient in creative thinking.

Problem solving. In problem solving, a problem or dilemma situation is identified, information gathered in answer to the problem, an hypothesis developed, the hypothesis is evaluated and modified if need be.

Analogizing. To be able to draw analogies is important. Thus, parallels may be drawn between and among cultures/ nations studied, even though differences do exist. But, the differences are not antonyms, but rather relationships may be observed. Many decisions in life are made through the use of rational thinking. Human reason based on knowledge is vital in ongoing units of study. It is important then for pupils to use knowledge in one way or another so that learning does not stress gaining inert ideas. Thus, knowledge may serve practical, recreational, creative, and theoretical purposes (See Ediger and Rao 2002).

A third category of objectives stresses the affective dimension. These kinds of ends emphasize quality attitudes, values, and feelings for pupils to develop. Good attitudes, for example, might stress the following:

- getting along well with others.
- accepting others as having extreme worth.
- using quality human relations approaches in relating well to others.
- assisting others as needed so that each may achieve optimally.
- using language appropriately to achieve objectives, rather than to develop ill will (See National Council for the Social Studies, 2001).

The social studies teacher then must have standards available for all to acquire so that proper behaviour in the classroom might result. Each standard needs to be clarified to become meaningful to learners. Pupils need to know which is/is not acceptable behaviour in the classroom and in society.

Organisation of the Social Studies Curriculum

There are selected ways of organizing units of study in social studies. The oldest approach is the separate subjects pattern. Here, history, for example, alone provides content for ongoing lessons and units. Most social studies educators prefer that subject matter be more connected in designing the curriculum. Thus, geography might be *correlated* with history. Historical events are then taught as occurring in a geographical region. To further relate social science disciplines, the teacher may stress *fusion*. History and geography then may be taught as being related to political science. The type of government of a particular nation/state may then be studied. To further emphasize fusion, economics may be brought into ongoing lessons and units of study. Thus, the economic system of a particular nation might then be taught as related to history, geography, and political science (See Curriculum Advice, 1994). The social studies may also be organised in which all disciplines are brought in to the unit of study such as science, mathematics, art, music, and physical education. Scientific developments such as the great Italian scientist Galileo occurred in a specific period of time such as the 1600s with his experiments pertaining to falling objects from the leaning tower of Pisa. History may not be understood well, of course, unless scientific developments, past and present, are brought into the teaching of social studies.

Social studies educators stress the importance of pupils perceiving knowledge as being related, as compared to the separate subjects approach, due to the following reasons:

- pupils retain learnings longer.
- pupils perceive the relationship of knowledge whereas the social scientist may perceive

separation of an academic speciality due to its depth study.

- pupils when engaging in problem solving use whichever academic discipline is needed to arrive at solutions.

Sequence in the Social Studies

The social studies teacher needs to be aware of the sequence or order of learning opportunities presented to pupils to optimize achievement. A pupil centred sequence may be stressed. Here, the learner with teacher guidance orders his/her own experiences. For example, in reading a unit related social studies library book, the pupil sequences ideas as they are being read. Or in viewing a related AV aid, the pupil achieves order in content being presented through viewing successive open ended scenes. When teacher/pupil planning is being used within a unit of study, the learner is heavily involved in sequencing experiences. The objectives, learning opportunities, and appraisal procedures may then be cooperatively planned by pupils with the assistance of the teacher. A psychological sequence is then in evidence.

Toward the other end of the continuum, the social studies teacher may solely determine the sequence of established objectives, learning activities, and evaluation procedures with little/no pupil input. With the teacher being the decision maker, a logical sequence is being emphasised (Ediger and Rao, 2001, Chapter Two).

Methods to Teaching Social Studies

There are a plethora of methods which may be used in teaching the social studies. Methods used need to be developmentally appropriate and meet the personal needs of pupils. The following are examples of methods to be considered in teaching a specific set of pupils:

Explanation. Explanations need to be given as necessary in an ongoing lesson and unit of study. Young children have a short attention span and cannot benefit from lengthy explanations as can upper elementary age pupils. The teacher must observe learners carefully to notice when to change from the use of explanations to a different method of teaching.

Problem solving. Problem solving is important in school and in society and thus needs thorough emphasis in the social studies. It takes time to stress quality problem solving procedures in the curriculum, but it has its many values.

Inductive method. From specifics, pupils are guided to come up with a generalisation. A questioning approach is used to help pupils arrive at a generalisation. The Socratic method, named after Socrates of ancient Athens, is another name for the inductive approach in learning.

Deductive method. Here, pupils are presented with a generalisations and are to achieve related, supportive specifics or details. From the general to the specific is a good clarifier of the deductive method of instruction.

Project methods. Here, the pupils with teacher help plan and make items and objects directly related to the ongoing social studies lesson or unit of study. A hands on procedure in learning is involved with constructing, doing, and making. A laboratory method is another way of describing the project method (See Ediger and Rao, 2000, Chapter Two).

A variety of methods should be used to teach pupils. If pupils attention should wane in a lesson, the teacher may then change to a different method of teaching. Along with the methods of instructions, the social studies teacher may also choose suitable experiences for pupil engagement in the social studies curriculum. Among others, these experiences may include the following within a social studies unit of study:

- reading from the basal textbook, library books, and other print sources.
- dramatizing what has been read (See Emery, 1992).
- constructing models of what is being studied.
- taking excursions which clarify major concepts and generalisations in the social studies.
- writing diary entries, and doing journal writing covering learnings acquired.
- giving individual and committee oral reports on selected social studies topics.
- developing a related mural, individual drawings, and/or water colour illustrations.
- making a relief map or model globe using paper' mache.
- doing a flow, organisational, vocabulary, and/or classification chart.
- developing models to indicate what has been learned.

The above named learning activities need to be developmental together with the appropriate method (s) of instruction. For example, if reading from the textbook is chosen as the learning activity for pupils to pursue with an inductive procedure or method of instruction, then the teacher needs to guide pupils to use the specifics in content read to arrive at a suitable generalisation. The generalisations must be supported by specifics or facts (See Banks, 1997).

Assessment of Achievement in the Social Studies

Diverse procedures need to be used to assess pupil achievement. A single approach is not adequate. Different assessment procedures evaluate diverse facets of a learner's achievement. Thus, a paper/pencil test may assess cognitive leanings such as understanding facts, concepts, and generalisations. Pupil progress in quality attitudinal development cannot be measured adequately with paper/pencil tests, but rather be assessed continually through teacher observation. In addition to required state mandated tests, the following may be used to notice pupil achievement:

- true/false, multiple choice, completion, essay, and matching test items. Validity and reliability are salient in test writing.
- teacher observation of pupil attitudes, social development, and emotional growth in ongoing activities.
- rubric use to assess the quality of discussions, construction work, and art endeavours as related to social studies units of instruction.
- journal writing to assess the quality of committee work.
- diary entries written to show individual achievement in goal attainment within ongoing daily lessons.
- pupil self appraisal in terms of desired criteria.
- use of performance assessment.
- pupil portfolio development.

Each of the above named assessment techniques has its place to assess learner achievement and progress. Thus teacher written test items such as true/false cannot measure the affective development of pupils, but teacher observation may be used to determine achievement in learner development of positive feelings toward others.

Assessment should relate directly to the objectives of instruction. It should pinpoint which objectives have/have not been achieved by pupils. Feedback from assessment results provide the teacher with knowledge of what needs to be emphasised in teaching and learning situations. Diagnostic approaches may then be used in that the teacher may remediate what pupils have not attained. The objectives of social studies instruction need to be clearly stated so that assessment may ascertain that which has/has not been acquired. Authentic tasks need to be in evidence, as learning opportunities, to measure pupil achievement. Multiple assessment procedures should be used to notice and verify pupil achievement. Pupils should high standards but the standards need to be achievable (See Wiggins, 1993).

Educational Psychology in the Teaching of Social Studies

Principles of learning taken from educational psychology have much to offer teachers in assisting pupils to achieve more optimally. These principles of learning are to be inherent with the methods of teaching being used as well as the subject matter taught. Also, the objectives, learning opportunities, and the assessment procedures are all interrelated and the principles of learning must become an integral part here, in teaching and learning situations.

To guide pupils to achieve well, the teacher, first of all, needs to guide learners to be actively engaged in ongoing learning experiences. To be engaged is to be interested in ongoing presentations. With a variety of activities, the teacher may change to a different activity before engagement starts to wane. Interested pupils learn more as compared to those who lack interest.

Second, pupils need to perceive reasons for learning. Reasons for leaning involve perceiving purpose for active participation in the tasks being presented. With purposes inherent, pupils become increasingly more motivated.

Third, pupils need to perceive meaning in each learning experience. Meaning pertains to understanding what is being taught. It also stresses that the pupil accepts the worth-whiteness of learning and achieving.

Fourth, pupils individually possess different styles of learning. Learning styles theory (Searson and Dunn, 2001) has much to offer the teacher in helping pupils achieve objectives of instruction. Vital ingredients here include the following:

1. acceptable noise levels, temperature readings, and informal versus formal seating arrangements.
2. emotional elements such as conformity versus non-conformity, as well as preferences for structure versus choice in terms of what to learn.
3. sociological factors such as studying alone or with others as well as preferring collegial versus a more authoritarian teacher.
4. physiological factors such as using auditory, factual, and/or kinesthetic ways of learning. Included are moving around or sitting still as well as eating versus not eating, while concentrating on the involved task.
5. psychological factors such as analytic learners who focus on facts in a step by step fashion which leads to an understanding, as compared to global learners who desire to understand what is learned and then how it relates to themselves before focusing on facts. Analytic learners respond best to printed words whereas global learners respond better to illustrations and pictures.

REFERENCES

1. Banks, James A. (1997), *Educating Citizens in a Multicultural Society*. New York: Teachers College Press.
2. Curriculum Advice (1994), *Geography for Life; National Geography Standards*. Washington, DC: National Council for Geographic Education.
3. Emery, Donna W. (1992), *"Children"s Understanding of Story Characters,"* Reading Improvement, 29 (1), 2-9.

4. Ediger, Marlow (2002), *"The Teaching of Social Studies,"* Edutracks, 1 (6) 6-11.
5. Ediger, Marlow, and D. Bhaskara Rao (2001), *Teaching Social Studies Successfully*. New Delhi, India: Discovery Publishing House, Chapter One.
6. Ediger, Marlow, and D. Bhaskara Rao (2001), *Teaching Science Successfully*. New Delhi, India: Discovery Publishing House, Chapter Two.
7. Ediger, Marlow, and D. Bhaskara Rao (2000), *Teaching Reading Successfully*. New Delhi, India: Discovery Publishing House, Chapter Two.
8. Ediger, Marlow, and D. Bhaskara Rao. *Teaching Social Studies in Elementary Schools*. New Delhi, India: Discovery Publishing House.
9. National Council for the Social Studies (2001), *Curriculum Standards for Social Studies*. Washington, DC: NCSS, pp. 3-6. Excerpted from the original by Walter C. Parker, and John Jarolimek.
10. Parker, Walter C. (2001), *Social Studies in Elementary Education*. Upper Saddle River, New Jersey: Merrill, Prentice Hall, Chapter Four.
11. Searson, Robert, and Rita Dunn (2001), *"The Learning Styles Teaching Model,"* Science and Children, 38 (5), 22-26.
12. Wiggins, Grant (1993), *Assessing Student Performance:* Exploring the Purpose and Limits of Testing. San Francisco: Jossey-Bass.

13

Reading, Mathematics, and Thought

Reading across the curriculum is salient to emphasize. The mathematics curriculum certainly can provide its many contributions in helping pupils in learning to read and read well. When teaching on the junior high school level, the author noticed that many pupils could not do word problems well because of reading problems. Mathematics does have its own unique vocabulary as well as words which cut across all academic disciplines. It also has abstract symbols which belong to mathematics solely. Words and symbols need to be read meaningfully by pupils. The following words are in common use in mathematics: addition, subtraction, multiplication, division, commutative, associative, distributive, algebra, equations, among many others. Common symbols which pupils need to read in an understanding manner include the following: "-," "+," "x," "<," among a plethora of others. Along with reading, mathematics teaching stresses the use of a variety of learning opportunities to guide pupils to attain worth while objectives. Developmental concrete, semiconcrete, and abstract experiences are needed to provide for individual differences among pupils in the classroom. Each needs to achieve as optimally as possible.

Reading and Word Problems

The adopted basal textbook in mathematics provides many learning opportunities for pupils. A the same time, it is difficult to appreciate by many pupils unless a considerable amount of help is given by the teacher to make subject matter meaningful. Word problems, in particular, may prove complex for many to solve.

Recognition of selected words might indeed cause difficulties for those who read below grade level. The teacher may read aloud those word problems causing difficulties to a small group of pupils. It is imperative that these pupils follow along in their basals as the content is being read aloud. By looking carefully at each word read aloud, the pupil can learn to identify new words and have them become a part of the child's basic sight vocabulary. The next time that these same words are met in print, hopefully the learner will be able to recognize each immediately. Peer teaching might also be used in that a good reader reads aloud the word problems from the text to others in the small group who need this assistance. Rearranging pupils into small groups for necessary instructional purposes may be done quietly and quickly so as not to interrupt others. The regrouping should also be done so as not to defame or minimize any pupil. Pupils need to feel accepted and have feelings of belonging within a group. They need to be given the best instruction possible. Many times, a slow reader can solve word problems correctly after the words become meaningful.

The teacher might assist pupils who have difficulties in word identification by giving instruction in the use of contest clues. A pupil might be substituting a ridiculous word for an unknown word. Here, the teacher must guide the pupil to make rational choices as to using sensible words in place of the unknown. Should this not be adequate, the pupil's attention should be placed upon the initial consonant of the unknown word. Many consonants are consistent between symbol (grapheme) and sound (phoneme). The help given pupils in using context clues and phonics should assist pupils to achieve more optimally in mathematics. If more assistance is needed in identifying unknown words, the teacher, perhaps, should give help in pupils looking at ending consonants to identify the unknown word and medial vowel letters.

Reading of sentences in mathematics might cause difficulties due to a lack of concentration by the pupil.

For example, when supervising university student teachers in the public schools, the author noticed pupils who could pronounce most of the words correctly in word problems, but did not comprehend that which was read. Concentration on the task at hand is very important and the teacher needs to assist pupils to comprehend what is read. This can be done by asking the pupil the meaning of subject matter read. This will take time since the pupil has not related reading to comprehending. Word calling is then in evidence. Calling words has little relevance unless the learner understands subject matter read. By working with the child, he/she can learn to comprehend and not only call words. An aide or a high school student in Future Teachers of America may also assist in having the word caller say his/her own words that which was read.

Once correct word identification and comprehension are there, pupils may need assistance in determining what is asked for in the word problem. A word problem may have several steps to pursue in having the learner arrive at a successful answer or solution. Each of these steps need analyzing in coming up with a correct answer. Creativity is then needed to synthesize, after analyzing the contents of the problem. Pupils need to be taught reasons for analysis, synthesis, and creativity in problem solving. Once the rationale is taught to pupils, it is easier to perceive reasons for engaging in each step of problem solving. These reasons or purposes need to be uppermost in the minds of children. The teacher can teach pupils to use mathematics in a mechanical way, but then difficulties accrue in not being able to solve problems when unique ways have been used in writing these problems. Problem solving should stress something novel which causes pupils to think. Thinking involves facing a perplexity in which "the tried and true" which have been used previously might not work, but there is still a pattern involved in problem solving in that:

- the problem needs clear identification. Information for the problem must be selected which will make for a possible solution.
- an hypothesis is developed based on information acquired.
- the hypothesis is tentative and needs checking.
- if upheld, the hypothesis stands as is. If not, the hypothesis is rejected and needs modification and change (Ediger and Rao, 2003, Chapter Twelve).

Criteria for Mathematics Teaching

There are selected criteria which need emphasizing in ongoing mathematics units of study:

- Each word problem should be made as concrete as possible with markers, diagrams, and drawings used to make subject matter meaningful.
- adequate readiness should be provided for an ensuing learning opportunity. The readiness provides the necessary background information for problem solving.
- appropriate sequence must be provided so that each previous learning provides background

information for the new subject matter encountered.

- active engagement of learners is needed so they might benefit more optimally from the new content. A hands on approach in developing mathematics concepts and generalisations should be stressed.
- interest in learning must be acquired so that pupils enjoy and appreciate mathematics as an academic branch of knowledge.
- purpose in problem solving should be stressed so that each pupil sees and perceives the "why" for problem solving.
- the needs of learners must be met in terms of developing feelings of belonging, security, and esteem. Pupils have feelings whereby they desire to be treated as human beings having worth when working individually, in small groups, and in the class as a whole.
- understanding of what is taught is a must; otherwise, subject matter could be committed to memory and soon forgotten in whole or in part.
- application of what has been learned is important. Pupils must perceive that subject matter learned is useful, rather than being learned for its own sake.
- self assessment of progress in mathematics is salient. The pupil then determines what is known and what is left to learn.
- reflective thinking needs adequate emphasis so that the pupil rehearses that which has been learned. These learnings will be remembered more thoroughly due to review involving mathematical learnings.

- logical thinking is an important goal in mathematics thinking. Much work in mathematics involves logical thought (Ediger and Rao, 2000, Chapter Eighteen).

The teacher needs to follow the above named criteria in teaching pupils so that each might well achieve as optimally as possible. The achievement should focus on objectives for pupil attainment.

Objectives, Testing, and Mathematics Achievement

Each state, except lowa, has mandated objectives for pupils to achieve. These objectives are generally available to teachers as benchmarks for instruction. The teacher selects the learning opportunities to align with the stated objectives. The state has developed mandated test to administer to pupils. They generally have been pilot tested to take out kinks or weaknesses. The accompanying tests need to match up with the accompanying objectives of instruction. If they do cover what is in the objectifies, then validity might well be in evidence. Reliability in the test items must also be in evidence in that there is consistency in each pupil's test results, in the pilot study, be it test/ retest, alternate forms, or split half reliability. The state mandated test are to be given in mathematics and in reading in grades 3-8, and 10.

State mandated objectives in mathematics are usually written in measurable terms. Either a pupil does/does not achieve any one objective as a result of instruction. The mathematics test contains considerable reading when word problems are listed. Computation also involves reading. There are numerals and mathematical symbols to read. Verbal and logical intelligences are used by pupils when taking the test. The state mandated tests would fit into being criterion referenced. The objectives have been written on the state level and are available to teachers to be used in instruction. These objectives are used as benchmarks for instruction. Theoretically many pupils can be successful and reach the top in goal achievement since the purpose of criterion referenced tests is not to spread pupils out on a continuum, but teachers are to assist pupils achieve optimally so the possibility for all to score high is possible. The objectives, available to pupils, are available to teachers to provide direction for instruction.

A few states use norm referenced, or standardised tests, whereby the pupils having taken the test are spread out from high to low. Thus, in pilot studies, the test writers, based on feedback from pupil test results, write multiple choice items which spread pupils out from the first to the ninety-ninth percentile. This makes it possible to make comparisons among school districts within a state. Those schools which have had high rates of pupil failure, based on state standards for two consecutive years in a row, might be taken over by the state.

The National Council for Teachers of Mathematics (NCTM) in 1989 developed a very comprehensive list of objectives for pupil attainment. These objectives may be used by the teacher as standards for pupils to achieve. The following are standards pertaining to numbers and numeration for pupils in kindergarten through grade four to achieve:

Standard six: number sense and numeration

In grades, K-4, the mathematics curriculum should include whole number concepts and skills so that pupils:

- construct number meanings through real world experiences and the use of physical materials
- understand our numeration system by relating counting, grouping, and place value concepts
- develop number sense
- interpret the multiple uses of numbers encountered in the real world (NCTM, 38).

In addition to reading word and computation problems, the following are good to use as manipulatives in hands on mathematics learning:

- attribute blocks consisting of different geometric shapes and colours
- interlocking counting cubes
- measuring instruments to determine length, width, area, volume, weight, and temperature readings.
- math boxes containing a variety of small objects and items to be used in counting, adding, subtracting, multiplying, and dividing.
- base ten place value charts, as well as base five and base two
- materials to use in teaching fractions such as circles, squares, and rectangles, to show halves, thirds, fourths, fifths, and eighths*
- play money (coins and bills)
- geometric models such as spheres, hemispheres, pyramids, rectangular solids, cubes, triangular solids, cones, and cylinders
- geoboards with nails hammered in plywood in a six by six array. A rubber band can be stretched around these nails to make a rectangle, square, and triangle, among others
- calculators, computers with accompanying software pertaining to tutorials, analysis and remediation, drill and practice, games, and simulation
- protractors and compasses (See Kennedy and Tipps, 1991).

A variety of developmental learning opportunities need to be in the offing for pupils. There may be teacher directed leanings for pupils, teacher/pupil planning of experiences, as well as individual pupil choices as to what to learn when selections are made from learning centres. A relaxed environment must be there, so that pupils may achieve and not worry or feel uneasy about the classroom climate. The teacher is there to encourage, assist, and help pupils achieve and make progress.

REFERENCES

1. Ediger, Marlow, and D. Bhaskara Rao (2000), *Teaching Mathematics Successfully*. New Delhi, India: Discovery Publishing House, Chapter Eighteen.
2. Ediger, Marlow, and D. Bhaskara Rao (2003), *Elementary Curriculum*. New Delhi, India: Discovery Publishing House, Chapter Twelve.
3. Ediger, Marlow, and Digumarti Bhaskara Rao (2004), *Teaching Mathematics in Elementary Schools*. New Delhi, India: Discovery Publishing House.
4. Kennedy, Leonard M., and Steve Tipps (1991), *Guiding Children's Learning of Mathematics*. Belmont, California: Wadsworth Publishing Company, Chapter Three.
5. NCTM (1989), *Curriculum and Evaluation Standards for School Mathematics*. Reston, Virginia: NCTM, 38.

Vocabulary Development and the Curriculum

Pupils need to continually strengthen their vocabularies. Why? A person can communicate more accurately by possessing a rich vocabulary be it in listening, speaking, reading, and writing. Then too, pupils need a well developed vocabulary which is integrated across the entire curriculum. People are limited what they can learn if a weak vocabulary is in the offing. What is listened to then just does not make sense in selected cases. An improved listening vocabulary improves comprehension of diverse ideas presented by the speaker. The chances are that the improved listening vocabulary makes for more effective oral communication. What one hears then can make for an improved speaking vocabulary. Words in oral communication might then be more precise and accurate in the spoken phase of learning. Listening and speaking effectively can make for background learnings necessary to develop reading proficiency. Quality reading does not occur in a vacuum, but is dependent upon rich personal experiences, gained through listening and speaking. A good reading vocabulary should then be in the offing. The listening, speaking, and reading vocabularies form the basis for having something to write about. Ideas are badly needed when writing subject matter for others to read.

Vocabulary Development Across the Curriculum

There are a plethora of vocabulary terms in the diverse curriculum areas. Social studies, as a curriculum area, has many vital and relevant vocabulary terms for pupils to master and use contextually. There are selected social science disciplines which provide content for the social studies. These, generally, include history, geography, political science, economics, anthropology, and sociology. In a unit on "The Middle Ages, vital vocabulary terms for pupils to attach meaning to in history include manor, noblemen, slave, serf, oath, knighthood (page, squire, knight), the guild (apprentice, journey man, master), castle, moat, draw bridge, and horsemanship.

In geography within the social studies, the following are relevant for pupil mastery: latitude, longitude, meridians, parallels, degrees, time zones, map projections, globes, arctic, antarctic, equator, as well as North and South Pole. Vital political science vocabulary terms include state and federal government, Bill of Rights, voting, candidates, democracy, citizenship, community service, civic responsibilities, laws, executive, judicial, and congress. Economics vocabulary deemed worthy for pupil study include the following: goods, services, economy, assembly line, cost efficient, automation, robots, consumer wants and needs, capitalism, socialism, choice, gross national product (GNP), labour, management, markets, and workers. Anthropology and sociology vocabulary terms include: culture, customs, socioeconomic levels, norms, folkways, mores as well as other human made parts of the environment (music, art, sports, architecture, food, clothing, and language (Ediger, 2000, Chapter Thirteen).

Vocabulary development must be emphasised across the curriculum. Each of the above named concepts should be studied and developed indepth by pupils. Depth teaching may stress a deductive approach. With deduction, clear and concise explanations must be given. It is good to use, when feasible, concrete and semi-concrete materials of instruction when the related vocabulary concept is being discussed. A lecture, as a deductive approach is not recommended due to the length and lack of meaning when using this approach.

With inductive learning, the teacher, for example, raises a question such as "What is meant by the concept *culture?* A brain storming session may be held and each response from pupils written on the chalkboard. An important rule is to listen carefully and not duplicate answers given. One pupil at a time may respond and all responses need to be respected. After pupils have run out of responses, the pupils might well summarize the ideas written on the chalkboard. Ultimately, a general definition may be secured of what is meant by "culture." If pupils did not respond with meaningful possibilities, the teacher may use a deductive method with more explanations and increased direction in terms of what pupils are to learn in vocabulary development. Inductive learning emphasizes the following methods:

1. it is pupil centred with ideas for teaching and learning coming from children with teacher guidance.
2. It is largely paced by pupils in terms of sequential learning.
3. It is based on using a variety of materials of instruction such as the concrete, the semiconcrete, and the abstract. Using the concrete (actual objects, realia, and items to refer to the vocabulary term), the semi-concrete (illustrations, pictures, filmstrips, slides, films, videotapes, and video disks), and the abstract (cassette recordings, discussions, reports, written work, listening, and reading) should all occur simultaneously, if possible. For example, the author likes to show a

model and a series of slides for pupils to understand "Mosque" as a vocabulary term. The teacher may not have a model (the concrete) to show the meaning of a vocabulary term, but can show one or more pictures (the semiconcrete) pertaining to the vocabulary term being discussed (the abstract). The teacher needs to be certain that pupils are attending and paying attention to the ongoing learning opportunity in vocabulary development as well as toward other learnings.

Deductive learnings are more teacher centred as compared to inductive methods. With deduction, the teacher needs to have ample concrete and semi-concrete materials to use in sequence. There will be less feedback from pupils with deductive approaches in teaching as compared to induction. The teacher needs to be certain that pupils are paying *much* attention to the ongoing learning opportunity in vocabulary development, as well as toward all instruction. Pacing must be done on what appears to be situations in which pupils respond to questions which the teacher raises. Pupils responding to questions provides needed feedback to the teacher as to what has' has not been learned. Pupils should be able to meaningfully define words as well as use them properly in a contextual manner. Developing a personal vocabulary notebook is useful to many pupils wherein newly encountered words are listed alphabetically with the definition given for each as well as the word being presented within sentence form. New words may be added to the notebook as they are learned. Pupils then feel rewarded as the number of new vocabulary words are mastered in meaning and use. This notebook becomes a handy reference source for the learner (Ediger and Rao, 2003, Chapter Eleven).

Terms which need special attention in social studies are the following:

1. technical terms which are peculiar to an academic discipline but used very infrequently in other

subject matter areas such as latitude and longitude in geography.

2. figurative terms such as "political platform." This term does not apply to standing on a platform, but stresses what, for example, are key beliefs which either democrats or republicans stand for during an election season.

3. words with multiple meanings such as "revolution." A revolution can occur in new ideas adopted and implemented, as well as an actual war, like the revolution of the American colonists against the British, 1776-1781.

4. terms peculiar to a given locality such as the prairies, borough, butte, mesa, and potlatch.

5. words confused with other words such as principal and principle, conservation with conversation, capital with capitol, and state for nation.

6. acronyms which are abbreviated expressions such as NATO, OPEC, UNICEF, and NOW.

7. quantity terms such as "soon after," "several years later," and MADD (Parker, 2001).

It is important for pupils to reflect upon vocabulary terms acquired. By reflecting upon these words, they become a part of the pupil. Use is made of these terms in a variety of ways. The more useful they become, the sooner new vocabulary terms become a part of the learner. A major goal of pupils should be to extend and learn indepth that which has value and is utilitarian. New vocabulary words acquired should be:

1. relevant according to the developmental level of the child.

2. challenging to the learner.

3. valuable and meet the personal needs of the pupil.
4. purposeful and possess reasons for their learning.
5. presented in an interesting manner.
6. acquired in a contextual setting.
7. used in a variety of settings.
8. achieved in situations involving a personal style of learning.
9. acquired across the curriculum.
10. applied in school as well as in the societal arena (See also, Piro, 2002).

Developing the Science Vocabulary

In diverse science lessons and units of study, the teacher needs to select new vocabulary terms, for pupil mastery, which are developmental and useful. The following should be acquired meaningfully within the framework of meeting learner needs.

1. cells (the basic unit of life), monera (bacteria, blue green algae), protists (tiny plants and animals called plankton, blue and brown algae, englenas, protozoans, amebas), Fungi (yeasts, molds, mushrooms, antibiotics).
2. plants—mosses, ferns, seed plants (angio sperms and gymnosperms).
3. animals without backbones (sponges, jelly fish and portuguese man of war; worms—flat, round, and segmented; mollusks—oysters, clams, snails, squids, and octopus; joint legged—crayfish, shrimp, and crabs; spiders, ticks, and mites; and insects with three pairs of legs, as well as having a head, thorax, and abdomen), and spiny skinned animals—sea urchins, sand dollars, and sea cucumbers.

4. animals with backbones—fish (scaly skins, two chambered heart, breath through gills and later through lungs, cold blooded, and lay shelless eggs.); amphibians (frogs, toads, newts, snakes, and salamanders) have three chambered hearts, are cold blooded, live in water and on land; reptiles have lungs, have three or four chambered heart, scaly skin, and lay eggs covered with a thick shell. Birds have four chambered hearts, breath with the use of lungs, possess feathers, and have the highest body temperature reading of all animals. Hawks, owls, eagles, and ospreys are birds of prey and keep vermin, among other small animals, down in number, Mammals—warm blooded, possess hair sweat glands, and nurse their young. They are the only vertebrates to possess a diaphragm, and have the most complex brain structure of all mammals. Some are meat eaters (lions, tigers, and wolves) while others are plant eaters (cow, camel, horse) (Blough and Schwartz).

Vocabulary terms in science must be selected carefully so that pupils achieve vital learnings. The learnings must be ordered properly with concrete, semiconcrete, and abstract learnings, along with the following guidelines for teaching and learning:

1. a hands on approach needs to be used in the instructional area with pupil involvement in experiments and demonstration. Careful observation is necessary to science phenomenon:

2. salient facts, concepts, and generalisations should be emphasised in ongoing lessons and units of study.

3. inductive procedures should be stressed heavily in the instructional arena.

4. written work should reflect the outcomes of pupil achievement such as in journal writing, diary entries kept, reports written, outlines developed, and logs kept of ongoing learning activities.
5. literature read should come from diverse sources such as the basal textbook, library books, reference books, and journals.
6. listening skills need further development such as in comprehending adequately ideas from discussions, committee work, cassette recordings, DVDs, and CD ROMs.
7. skills need to be adequately achieved in individual, small group, and large group work. An attitude of caring and assisting others to achieve well is inherent.
8. wanting to learn more in science is a vital affective end for pupil achievement.
9. showing optimal quality in doing science in the curriculum.
10. assessing the self in terms of recommended standards and using the results as feedback to improve learning and achievement (Ediger and Rao 2001, Chapter Three).

Developing a Mathematics Vocabulary

The mathematics vocabulary of pupils is generally developed within the subject matter being discussed. For example, the following vocabulary terms are acquired in ongoing discussions as pupils are achieving new objectives: addend, sum, minuend, subtrahend, difference, factor, product, dividend, divisor, and quotient, point, line, line segment, ray, sets, subsets, square root, cube root, length, width, area, volume, square, triangle, rectangle, parallelogram, circle, rhombus, cube, rectangular solid, triangular solid, cone, pyramid, cylinder. Pupils need to understand each vocabulary term indepth within the framework of seeing a visual representation of the geometrical figure, as it is being discussed. Depth teaching indicates that a pupil use a mathematics term in a variety of developmental situations. Uses of vocabulary terms can be made in discussions, in peer and committee work, in problem solving activities, in games, and in society.

Intellectuals and thinkers all over the world view education as a crucial factor in raising the standard of living all over the globe. Education being a sub-system of the larger social order is always under review for adjustment. This process is accelerated today because of the very fast changes which are occurring in various directions. A serious review and transformation of the ongoing educational systems in various parts of the world is unavoidable for the very survival of man. With its ramification, the transition from the traditional to the futuristic setting is not so easy. It has thrown many challenges to the educational planners, particularly in the third world. In spite of it, striving for excellence in education has marked the efforts a reorganisation everywhere for the past decade or two (Premila, 2001).

Quality objectives, learning opportunities, and assessment procedures need to be carefully chosen and implemented.

A variety of assessment procedures need to be used since each approach is a check on the other. Thus state mandated, as well as teacher written tests may be used such as essay, multiple choice, true-false, completion, and matching. Daily evaluation results may become a part of a portfolio developed by the pupil with teacher guidance. The portfolio with its randomised compilation of pupil work might then be shared with parents so that the latter may notice how to assist the child to achieve more optimally.

Computer use of routine scoring of objective test items saves teacher time and talent for actual teaching. Computerised scoring, though, has its weaknesses:

A Massachusetts social studies teacher who caught a mistake on the state's assessment exams is a new hero in the eyes of hundreds of 8th graders.

John J. Gibbons Jr., a 49 year old social studies teacher at Clinton Middle School in Clinton, Massachusetts, discovered a question on the Massachusetts Comprehensive Assessment System 8th grade history exam which had two correct answers. The multiple choice question asked students to identify the powers granted to congress by the US Constitution. Two correct answers—enacting laws and collecting taxes—were listed. But when the exam was scored, only the choice for enacting laws was deemed correct.

Mr. Gibbons contacted the department and explained the error. Now 666 students who thought they had failed the exam had their scores bumped to passing, and about 14,000 who took the test will see their scores increase (Gehring, 2002).

Reading and the Language

Vocabulary development in the language arts is vital in order for pupils to become increasingly proficient in listening, speaking, reading, and writing. These four vocabularies cut across all academic and curriculum areas. There are a variety of ways to assist pupils in vocabulary development in contextual situations within the reading/ language arts connection such as:

1. reading orally to pupils.
2. having pupils engage in discussions.
3. participating in ongoing activities at the listening centre optimal achievement. Learning opportunities

need selection which guide pupils in achieving the stated intents. Evaluation of pupil achievement in vocabulary achievement should be ongoing and continuous.

REFERENCES

1. Blough, Glen O., and Julius Schwartz (1984), *Elementary School Science and How to Teach It,* Seventh Edition. New York: Holt, Rinehart and Winston, Chapters Ten A and B.
2. Ediger, Marlow, and D. Bhaskara Rao (2002), *Teaching Language Arts Successfully.* New Delhi, India: Discovery Publishing House.
3. Ediger, Marlow, and D. Bhaskara Rao (2003), *Language Arts Curriculum.* New Delhi, India: Discovery Publishing House, Chapter Nine.
4. Ediger, Marlow (2002)," *Assessing the School Principal," Education,* 123 (1), 90-95.
5. Ediger, Marlow, and D. Bhaskara Rao (2003), *Elementary Curriculum.* New Delhi, India: Discovery Publishing House, Chapter Eleven.
6. Ediger, Marlow (2000), *Social Studies Curriculum in the Elementary School.* Kirksville, Missouri: Simpson Publishing Company, Chapter Thirteen.
7. Gehring, John (2002), *Massachusetts Teacher Finds Error",* Hundreds Now Pass The Test," Education Week, October 9, p. 18.
8. Parker, Walter S. (2001) *Social Studies in Elementary Education.* Upper Saddle River, New Jersey: Prentice—Hall, Inc., 393.
9. Piro, Joseph M. (2002), *"The Picture of Reading; Deriving Meaning in Literacy Through Image,"* The Teading Teacher, 56 (2), 126-134.
10. Premila, K.S. (2002), *Effect of Computer Assisted Indstruction and Assessment in Learning Mathematics Among High School Students*—Gender Perspective. Kodaikanal, India: Mother Teresa Women's University, Ph D thesis evaluated by the author.

Testing and Measurement of Pupil Achievement

Students of education have noticed the tremendous emphasis being placed upon testing and measuring of student achievement. News media frequently criticizes pupil achievement in terms of test results achieved. It appears that these test scores cannot go high enough to please news reporters and writers of news items. Testing and measuring pupil achievement are sensitive items to accomplish. Teachers and school administrators may be very critical of items contained in a test. They also might well criticize the time allotted for giving the many tests to pupils as well as that more than a state mandated test needs to provide data on pupil achievement. One test then is not adequate to show what pupils have learned.

The author will analyze diverse procedures to appraise learner achievement using realism, existentialism, experimentalism, and idealism as different philosophies of appraisal.

Realism and Assessment of Student Progress

Realists believe that one can know the real world as it truly is, in whole or in part. Thus for example, chemists have identified 107 elements which make up the natural environment. Each compound can be stated in terms of the inherent elements. Sugar then contains the following elements: C_6 H_{12} O_6, C=carbon, H=hydrogen, and O=oxygen. The exact number of atoms in a molecule of sugar such is 6 atoms of carbon, 12 of hydrogen, and 6 of oxygen. Measurable amounts, involving accuracy, are in each compound, such as sugar.

The model of science and mathematics with its precision has the been applied to determining student achievement. Standardised tests such as The Lowa Test of Basic Skills are used to measure learner achievement and progress. There may be a single percentile given for student achievement from taking the total test. For each component part, such as mathematics, there may be a separate percentile from the other academic areas and skills as measured by The Lowa Test of Basic Skills. A percentile is a single numeral indicating how well the student is achieving.

When the measurement movement in education came forth in the early 1900s, E. L. Thorndike, Professor at Columbia University in New York City, stressed the thesis that "whatever exists, exists in some amount, and if it exists in some amount, it can be measured." Thorndike and his associates developed tests to measure handwriting progress, arithmetic achievement, and student learning in general. The measurement movement survived in time/ place and is extremely important presently to use in ascertaining student achievement. Pertaining to E. L. Thorndike, Thayer (1970) wrote: The early years of the twentieth century were conscious in the application of science to all phases of business and industry. It was applied to not merely the invention of new products and processes but to the details of organisation and management designed to promote economy and efficiency. Experts trained in scientific management studied carefully the performances of workers on the job with results so fruitful in economy and efficiency that many came to be seen in "job analysis" possibilities of application not only to vocational education but to the reform of other aspects of education as well. All that was needed it seemed, was to identify the specific outcomes by insuring that pupils engage in the activities certain to eventuate in the proper habits and skills, information, attitudes, ideals, and the like.

Realism as a philosophy of testing and measurement is very much in evidence in the following concepts: behaviourally stated objectives, measurement driven instruction (MDI), as well as report cards (to compare school districts in achievement within a state). Programmed learning strongly emphasizes the measurement movement such as in the following writing by Harris and Sipay (1985):

Programmed materials designed so that the user (1) encounters a series of small tasks in which success is very likely; (2) is involved in the learning process through actively responding; (3) perceives immediate feedback as to the correctness of each response. In theory, programmed materials should greatly facilitate individualised instruction because they allow each student to work almost independently with materials suitable for his or her needs, proceeding at a pace commensurate with ability and interest.

State departments of education, governors of states, as well as state senators and representatives have strongly recommended that each state establish standards (objectives) for students to attain. Tests are written to determine if the objectives, and how many, have been achieved by students. The recently passed legislation by the US House and Senate, signed by the President, as attached to the Elementary and Secondary Education Act (ESEA) emphasizes the following:

1. state mandated tests be developed which measure student achievement in the language arts, science, mathematics, and the social studies.

2. these tests are to be given in grades 3-8 and in grade ten.
3. student test results are to be broken down in terms of gender, race, and income levels. Students who fail the state mandated tests three years in a row will be given a voucher to attend a school of their choice. Educationally bankrupt schools whose students fail to achieve adequately on the state mandated tests may be taken over by the state.
4. information from test results are to be provided to teachers so they may use it to help students achieve more adequately on the next grade level.
5. gaps in student achievement between/among the races, income levels, and minority groups are to be eliminated.

Realism then as a philosophy of education emphasizes that measurable results from pupils can be obtained to state precisely how well a student is achieving. Comparisons may be made in ascertaining how well pupils and school districts are achieving within a state. Precise information from student test results make it possible to accurately compare one student with another as well as one school district with another.

Existentialism and Student Achievement

Existentialists believe that each person should learn to make choices, from among alternatives, in society. There should be no compulsion, ideally, in making these choices. In the school setting, then, pupils need to learn to make decisions. Decision making, for example, may involve the selection of reading materials in a programme of individualised reading. There needs to be an adequate number of library books on diverse genera for students when choosing what to read. With existentialist philosophy, the library books should contain content on the human experience in all of its manifestations. The dread to make many choices in life, the anxiety, the tensions. The fears, and the emotions which make a person human must be thoroughly reflected in the decisions made of what to read. The pupil, alone, needs to choose content to read and then share ideas gleaned in a conference with the teacher or with peers. The pupil needs to select what to discuss. The teacher may take notes on comprehension skills achieved by the learner. Comparisons may be made by the teacher with later conferences to notice pupil achievement. The teacher needs to notice how the pupil is achieving in the area of existentialist thinking. Such concepts as the following need to be understood and emphasised by the pupil: freedom, choice, dilemmas, human condition, death, living, dread, alienation awesomeness, and anxieties. A central idea in existentialist thought is the need to personally develop reasons for living; the purpose or reasons for living are not given to any individual but must be sought.

Existentialism does not Advocate

1. the use of predetermined objectives for pupil achievement, rather the objectives emerge within and from the individual.
2. testing to determine achievement, rather the pupil determines what to learn and which content to pursue. The teacher is a guide and stimulates learning.
3. external motivation, but rather believes the individual is motivated from within.
4. the learning of subject matter to the minimizing of pupils focusing upon the feelings or affective dimension of human beings. Rather, feelings are the most important part of the human condition.

5. objectivity of subject matter, but rather content acquired by the pupil is unique and *subjective* to the involved individual.

Pertaining to existentialist thinking, Harper (1955) wrote the following:

Existentialism, as the name implies, is a philosophy of human existence. It arose early in the nineteenth century in response to a cultural climate in which Soren Kierkegaard, observed that men had forgotten what it means to exist. Men had leaned what it means to be one in a crowd, to be a mass; they had forgotten what it means to be an individual, that is what it means to die, to suffer, to decide, to love. They had forgotten what it means to stand apart, as each man is born to stand apart, from the rest of the universe and from one's fellows...

Experimentalism and Pupil Achievement

Experimentalists believe that one cannot know ultimate reality as it truly is, but he/she can experience it. The experiences will not be perfect in knowing ultimate reality, but in degrees come close enough to what is reality so that the individual can function effectively in society. Experiences emphasize the need for change in society. With experiences, problems are identified which need solving. John Dewey (1859-1952) was a leading advocate of experimentalism as a philosophy of education. Among his many writings, Democracy and Education (Dewey, 1916) states his beliefs on teaching pupils. In his laboratory school at the University of Chicago, Dewey tried out his experimentalists beliefs in practical situations. Problem solving was a major method of instruction emphasised in the curriculum. Here, pupils with teacher assistance identified a problem in a contextual situation. The problem is delimited so that it possesses clarity. Information is gathered in answer to the problem. The information is analysed with critical thinking involved. An hypothesis results which is tentative and subject to testing in a life-like situation. The hypothesis is revised if necessary. Problem solving is stressed as being the complete act of thought.

Experimentalists believe in integrating school and society. Thus, What is important in society, such as problem solving, is also to be emphasised in the school curriculum. School and society are not to be separated, but become integrated entities.

Experimentalism believes in assessing pupils to do the following:

1. using subject matter to solve problems. Subject matter is not to be learned for its own sake, nor to achieve predetermined objectives.
2. identifying problem areas in context as the unit of study progresses.
3. acquiring facts, concepts, and generalisations as a problem area is being solved.
4. evaluation consists of using relevant sources of information to solve a problem as well as to test an hypothesis in a functional situation.
5. being actively involved in problem solving, not passive recipients of knowledge. Interest in learning makes for student effort in achieving, growing, and developing.

Pertaining to John Dewey, Atkinson and Maleska (1965) wrote the following:

To Dewey education has two sides—psychological and and social: neither may be subordinated or neglected. The Psychological nature of a child forms the basis for his education—it is the teacher's responsibility to make full use of his natural, spontaneous activities. Describing original nature as being spontaneously impulsive rather than passive, Dewey divided impulses into four kinds: The social impulses of communication or conversation; the constructive impulse to make things; the impulse to investigate things; and the impulse of artistic or creative expression.

With these impulses in mind, said Dewey, the school must be changed from a place of sedentary listening to one for active working or doing. The teaching process must be planned to allow the child to learn whatever possible by his own experiences and, in that way, to acquire the habit of thinking....

Idealism and Pupil Achievement

Idealists believe in a subject centred curriculum. Idealism might well have been called idea-ism since it advocates an idea centred curriculum. Worthwhile idea centered objectives need to be carefully selected for pupils to attain. One cannot know ultimate reality as it truly is, but persons can receive ideas from the natural and social environment. Mind is real and needs to be developed. An alert mind is necessary to attain ideas pertaining to the natural/social environment. Mental development is then of utmost importance since ideas are to be achieved by pupils. Generalisations are more important to learn as compared to learning specifics, although the specifics support the broad ideas. Ideas need achievement rather than direct knowledge pertaining to external world, which is unknowable. Idealists believe in selected concepts being apriori. That is to say that selected ideals (here, idealism has the connotation of stressing ideals to be achieved) have always been true in time and space. Words such as truth, honesty, goodness, beauty, justice, and courage, have been true apriori, or always. The *will* must be used to achieve the abstract, since interest alone on the student's part is not adequate. To make progress in learning might well emphasize doing the unpleasant.

To achieve ideas and ideals, reason is necessary on the part of the learner. The reasoning person develops ideas and ideals which transcend sense data. Beyond sense data (seeing, smelling, hearing, touching, and tasting) are purposes and values which assist to attain the ideals of the apriori. For many idealists beyond the here and the now is God. This life may not be the finality of one's deeds and acts. The here and the now may be a testing ground for the hereafter, also called heaven. Thus beyond sense perceptions, many vital happenings transpire. Human beings are at the apex of living things. They are much higher and more significant as compared to what is called animal life.

Idealism emphasizes the coherence theory in testing statements. Thus, a true statement is one which fits in logically with others. Reason is used to test the involved logic. Pertaining to idealism, Brubacher (1966) wrote:

The most prolific work on the idealistic philosophy of education in the twentieth century was Herman Harrrell Horne (1874-1946). At a time when idealism was rapidly fading as the dominant American theory of education, Horne managed to draw together the various strains of idealism into their more systematic educational exposition. In addition to much that is already familiar, he made two points of his own. One is his volition and effort in learning. The pupil is like a plant, he agreed with Friedrich Froebel, in that his reasons are self-active. But the child is unlike the plant, Horne continued, in that he can withhold his response. Hence the ultimate responsibility for getting an education rests on the will of the pupil. All education, therefore, is self education; it is the result of voluntary effort put forth by a self-active mind. If not, then like Immanuel Kant (1724-1804), Horne urged that the pupil put forth effort in obedience to what he *ought* to do.

Idealists believe in evaluating pupils to do the following:

1. expressing subject matter acquired clearly and accurately.
2. putting forth *much* effort in learning.
3. being able to use reason and logic effectively.
4. using quality ideas silently kin speaking and in writing.

5. placing high worth on eternal values (apriori) such as goodness, beauty, and truth. With adequate mental development, the individual may reach out to achieve these ideas and ideals.

Perennialism is a philosophy of education directly related to idealism. Perennialists believe in students studying he Great Books of the western world. These books contain the writings of great minds of the past and their ideas have stood the test of time and place. Recent writings do not contain the worth as do the classics. They have not, as yet, been determined as remaining important as the years have gone by. The writings of William Shakespeare, Robert, Louis Stevenson, Nathaniel Hawthorne, Henry Wadsworth Longfellow, among others, tower above those of recent endeavours in literature. Perennialism spokesperson, Mortimer Adler (1902-1998), developed his philosophy in The Paideia of which Tanner and Tanner (1990) wrote the following:

The perennialists refusal to consider the nature of the learner in developing he curriculum is reflected in the Paideia Proposal. Instead of seeing childhood and youth as distinct phases of human development requiring uniquely appropriately learning experiences for effective growth, childhood and youth are seen as being obstacles to be overcome as quickly as possible. "Youth itself is the most serious impediment—in fact, youth is an insuperable obstacle to being an educated person," declares the Proposal. The proposal goes on to call for twelve years of basic schooling for all, capped by the Socratic study of great literary works and other works of art. This kind of learning "aims at raising the mind up from a lesser or weaker understanding to a stronger and fuller one," declares Adler, and the "art of the teacher depends on the teacher's understanding of how the mind learns by the exercise of its own power," declares Adler, as though the mind exists as a separate entity.

Perennialism believes in assessing student achievement in the following ways:

1. achievement in acquiring ideas from classical writings.
2. active involvement of students in discussions pertaining to the *classics* by using the Socratic method of inquiry.
3. use of the mind or mental powers through the exercise of their own powers, such as in heavy student involvement in inductive learning. A questioning approach by the teacher needs to be used as an art, not a science, of teaching.

REFERENCES

1. Atkinson, Carroll, and Eugene T. Maleska (1965), *The Story of Education.* New York: Chilton Books, pp. 87-88.
2. Brubacher, John S., *A History of the Problems of Education.* New York: McGraw-Hill Book Company, pp. 128 and 129.
3. Dewey, John (1916), *Democracy and Education,* New York: The MacMillan Company.
4. Ediger Marlow and D. Bhaskara Rao (2003), *Philosophy and Curriculum.* New Delhi, India: Discovery Publishing House.
5. Harper, Ralph (1955), *"Significance of Existence and Recognition for Education,"* Modern Philosophies of Education. Chicago: The University of Chicago Press, p. 215.
6. Harris, Albert J., and Edward R. Sappy (1985), *How to Increase Reading Ability.* White Plains, New York: Longmans, Inc., p. 71.
7. Tanner, Daniel, and Laurel Tanner (1990), *History of the School Curriculum.* New York: The Macmillan Company, p. 333.
8. Thayer, V.T. (1970), *Formative Ideas in American Education,* New York: Dodd, Mead and Company, p. 224.

Teacher Involvement to Evaluate Achievement

Much is written about using standardised and state mandated tests to measure student growth in science. Little, however, is written about using teacher developed tests to measure student science achievement in the classroom. Too frequently, standardised tests and state mandated tests omit learner progress in the every day learnings in science achievement in the classroom. Teacher developed tests can be more valid and reliable then either standardised or state mandated tests. Standardised tests are global and do not have accompanying objectives for the teacher to use in teaching science. State mandated tests may have accompanying objectives which teachers may use to gauge their teaching. The teacher may then teach in a manner whereby the state mandated test might have rather high validity since what is taught may be tested when using the state mandated test. Selected states omit science content and skills in the mandated tests. The feeling then might well be that science is not as important as reading and mathematics, for example.

There is probably no better way to write valid test items than the classroom teacher doing the writing who knows and understands what has been taught in the classroom. The science teacher also has understandings of what the developmental level of the student is when writing appropriate test items. Thus, test items need to be written on the reading and understanding level of the students who are to take the test.

Too many teachers, however, are not acquainted with standards to use in test writing.

Standards for Test Writing

The National Research Council (NRC) has just released publication of *Classroom Assessment and the National Education Standards* (National Science Teachers Association, 2001). Six goals are listed in the introduction of this publication and these are the following:

- Articulate a research based rationale for helping teachers improve classroom assessment.
- Clarify the concept of effective classroom assessment.
- Provide illustrations and guides to the development and selection of assessment processes and tools.
- Assist teacher educators and staff developers who will include assessment in their work with prospective and practicing teachers.
- Address issues that school and district decisionmakers face in their efforts to improve classroom assessment.

What students learn each day in ongoing science lessons and units of study is important. A single percentile given to show student results on a standardised or state mandated test for an entire school year, or other selected interval of time, does not provide a comprehensive picture of the learner's achievement in science (Ediger, 1990, 241-246). To use either of these tests to reveal learner progress in science has the following weaknesses:

1. multiple choice test items are generally used for student responses to indicate what has been learned. These are paper/pencil test items to measure facts, concepts, and generalisations acquired by students. Major emphasis may be placed here upon measuring factual information achieved by students since this is the easiest kind of content to measure in a multiple choice test.
2. hands on approaches in science teaching and learning might well be greatly minimised or ignored since their strengths and weaknesses cannot be machine scored. A science teacher who has stressed a hands on approach in student learning in the classroom may find the multiple choice test items tend to measure verbal intelligences such as reading largely or only.
3. no exceptions may be made for individual differences among students. Thus all students have the same amount of allotted time to complete the standardised or state mandated test, all experience the same directions for test taking, all responses are assessed using the same answer key, and all respond to the same kind of test items. Selected students need more test taking time than do others as well as to have directions explained more thoroughly for taking the test. Then too, there may be more than one correct answer than what is presented in the assessment key. Reading multiple choice test items may not be a favourite way of revealing what has been learned in science. A handicapped student, especially, may need special accommodations.

4. science as a curriculum area may not appear on a state mandated test since major emphasis is being placed upon measuring reading and mathematics achievement. Standardised tests, if they do contain test items pertaining to science, may have too few test items pertaining to this vital area of academic achievement.
5. validity may well be lacking if the test stresses abstract learnings such as students reading and responding to multiple choice test items and the classroom teacher having emphasised concrete and semi-concrete approaches in teaching science.

A sampling of every day science achievement of students may be incorporated into a science portfolio. The portfolio, as an example, may contain the following entries:

1. snapshots of hands on approaches from ongoing lessons and units of study.
2. written work pertaining to summaries; outlines; book reports; as well as expository, creative, and narrative writings.
3. a video tape of collaborative endeavours of students to notice the quality of interactions.
4. tape recordings of oral presentations such as a book report.
5. drawings of construction items made for science experiments and demonstrations.
6. dramatisations, evaluated on a five point scale, pertaining to a unit on famous scientists, for example.
7. self evaluation of students in terms of quality criteria.
8. art products such as murals, diagrams, and other illustrations developed of what was studied in science units of study.

9. test results of classroom developed tests measuring achievement in ongoing units and lessons.

10. student/teacher planning of what is left to learn within a specific unit in science. A carefully designed rubric may be used to assess the quality of each portfolio (Ediger, 2001, 150-155).

Multiple Intelligences Theory

Multiple Intelligences Theory (Gardner, 1993) indicates that there are numerous possibilities for students to reveal in achievement. Here, students may use their own individual strengths to indicate achievement through the following ways:

1. verbal intelligences such as in reading and responding to test items.
2. logical intelligence as in reasoning to secure information.
3. musical/rhythmical such as in writing lyrics and putting the words to music to reveal what has been learned.
4. interpersonal intelligences whereby the strengths lie within the individual working by the self to indicate achievement from a lesson or unit of study.
5. interpersonal intelligences in which a learner best reveals learnings obtained through collaborative endeavours.
6. bodily/kinesthetic whereby the student indicates what has been learned through manual dexterity. There are a plethora of ways here for students to show achievement in science units such as in constructing models and objects, making science equipment, and doing projects.

7. scientific intelligences which is truly the heart of the science curriculum as in objective thinking about nature and the natural world.

The student with teacher guidance may select the approach(s) to be used to reveal what has been learned in science lessons and units of study. This puts more responsibility upon the student, rather than upon test writers far removed from the local classroom, in deciding how to be assessed to indicate achievement. Each of the above named intelligences possessed by a student may be used to show progress in the science curriculum.

To use multiple intelligences theory requires inservice education for teachers. Classroom teachers need to study, see models of multiple intelligences theory in operation to assess learner achievement, and eventually implement with mentor assistance diverse facets of this philosophy of evaluation. In service education is necessary then for teachers to be able to use new procedures in the assessment process.

Learning Styles Theory in the Assessment Process

Under which classroom environmental conditions do students achieve more optimally? Learning styles theory has much to offer in thinking about the learning environment for students in the classroom. Season and Dunn (2001) in their research have identified factors which assist or hinder individuals in the classroom in achieving as optimally as possible:

1. acceptable noise levels, temperature readings, as well as formal versus informal seating arrangements.

2. emotional elements such as conformity versus nonconformity, as well as preferences for choices as to what to learn.

3. sociological factors such as studying alone or with others as well as preferring collegial relations versus structure with a more authoritative teacher.

4. physiological factors such using auditory, tactual, and/or kinesthetic ways of learning. Included too are moving around or sitting still as well as eating versus not eating while concentrating on the task at hand.

5. psychological factors such as being an analytic learner who focuses on a step by step fashion which leads to an understanding, as compared to global learners who desire to understand what is learned and how it relates to themselves before focusing on facts. Analytic students respond best to printed words whereas global learners respond better to illustrations and pictures.

Workshops and faculty meetings are needed for teachers to become thoroughly familiar with learning styles theory of teaching and learning as well as using its components in the assessment procedure. Teachers need to consider learning styles theory when evaluating under which conditions students do best in achieving objectives in science instruction.

Written Tests in the Science Curriculum

There are selected criteria which need to be used by teachers in writing valid and reliable test items to measure learner achievement and progress. Quality test items then need to be in the offing for assessment results to be useful for the science teacher. Poorly written, vague items will not provide the useful information needed to design the science curriculum.

Which are Selected Criteria for the Teacher to Use?

Multiple choice test items are used very frequently by writers of standardised and criterion referenced tests. Teacher written multiple choice test items should possess the following:

1. they should contain a stem and four plausible responses. Four is not a magic number, but if there are three responses, then the student has a better chance of guessing the correct answer. If five responses are in the offing, it might be quite complex in writing each as being plausible or rational.

The following is a model multiple choice item:

Which is *incorrect* in naming the three states of matter?

(*a*) solids.

(*b*) rocks.

(*c*) gases.

(*d*) liquids.

There is only one correct answer in that rocks are not one of the three states of matter. The test item is quite factual. However, there are vital facts for students to understand and use in developing increasingly a more complex science vocabulary. Thus, there are a plethora of liquids, solids, and gases for students to encounter in a quality sequential curriculum. Then too relevant facts are the building blocks for higher levels of cognition.

2. no clues are to be given when the student encounters sequential multiple choice test items. Thus, test item number one should not provide a clue as to which is the correct response for test item number two, and others sequentially.
3. each stem needs to be grammatically correct with the four plausible responses:

Three major classification of rocks are:

(*a*) sandstone, basalt, and marble.

(*b*) igneous, metamorphic, and sedimentary.

(*c*) liquids, solids, and gases.

(*d*) conglomerate, magma, and shale.

4. the test items need to be arranged an ascending order of complexity. The reason for this being psychological in that the easier test items may build self confidence within students to tackle the increasingly more complex test items sequentially.
5. written test items must cover what has been taught in the classroom so that increased validity is in evidence.
6. peer review of test items may be advisable to take out the weaknesses in a multiple choice test.
7. balance among different topics covered in science instruction need to appear on the test. If environmental education has been taught in class for example, then related test items need to appear on the test. Face validity is then in evidence (Ediger, 1994, 1-4).
8. feedback from student test results should be used to pinpoint weaknesses and thus reteach that which is needed.
9. printouts of learner test results provide a basis for assessment of the quality of test items. If too many miss an item, perhaps it needs to be revised to make it more meaningful.
10. tests are an integral part of instruction and should be used to improve the curriculum, not to make comparisons among students. Learning opportunities should be used to encourage student progess in science (Ediger, 1994, 24-25).

Teacher Observation of Students in Science Achievement

Leadership is certainly needed from teachers and the school principal to use quality criteria to ascertain student achievement in science (Ediger, 1999, 1-5). Test results may well be worthless unless the standards used in measurement and evaluation to determine student science achievement possess face validity as well as reliability, such as test/retest, alternate forms and/or split half. There are a plethora of factors which need to be incorporated into the writing of quality tests including being on the present reading level of students who will be taking the test. Individual differences should be provided for including variable time limits for students individually who need more time to complete a test.

To harmonize a hands on approach in teaching/learning in science with the assessment process, the teacher may use observational techniques. The following criteria may be used in the observational process by the science teacher when students are doing hands on science:

1. how well a learner is identifying problems to solve in science.
2. how effective the student is in gathering information directly related to the problem.
3. how proficient the student is in achieving an hypothesis.
4. how well the learner does in testing and evaluating the worth of the hypothesis.
5. how capable the student is in modifying the hypothesis, if necessary.

Teacher observation may be used to determine how well a student is doing in each of the five above named categories. An additional vital item to observe is how well students are using science equipment and materials in problem solving experiences.

Metacognition in Science

Metacognition skills are important to use in the evaluation process. Metacognition deals with thinking about thinking. Early in the child's school experiences, he/she should be aided to achieve as optimally as possible (See

Allen, Spring, 2001). The science teacher needs to provide a model to assist students to reflect upon what has been achieved in science in an ongoing lesson or unit of study. This provides opportunities, not only to reflect upon what has been acquired, but also for the student to think about what is left to learn. Motivational factors arise here in that the learner feels a sense of accomplishment as well as there being more to achieve. Relating that which has been achieved with what is left to learn makes for connections of the older learnings with the new. Review within the reflection process is a powerful factor in retention of subject matter, skills, and attitudes, as well as creating a desire to continue achieving. Too frequently, individuals believe that what has been learned will remain there for retrieval. But forgetting and problems in retrieval are forthcoming. For metacognition to become an important factor in self evaluation, the student needs to

1. be responsible for his/her own achievement in science.
2. trust the self, with teacher guidance, to develop quality criteria in and for self evaluation.
3. lean upon the self to evaluate, assess, and accomplish.
4. monitor the self to determine if science goals of instruction are being achieved.
5. rehearse, analyze, and synthesize objectives, learning opportunities, and assessment procedures with each being vital in teaching and learning.

REFERENCES

1. Allen, Rick (2001), *"Cultivating Kindergarten, the Reach for Academic Heights Raises Challenges,"* Curriculum Update. Alexandria, Virginia: The Association for Supervision and Curriculum Development, p. 1.

2. Ediger, Marlow (2001), *"Assessment, Geography and the Student,"* Journal of Instructional Psychology, 28 (3), 150-155.
3. Ediger, Marlow (1994), *"Environmental Education and the Curriculum,"* School Science, 32 (1), 1-4. Published by the National Council for Educational Research and Training, in India.
4. Ediger, Marlow (1994), *"The Unexpected in Science,"* Investigating, 10 (3), 24-25. Published by the Australian Science Teachers Association.
5. Ediger, Marlow (1999), *"Leadership in the Science Curriculum,"* The Educational Review, 105 (11), 1-5.
6. Ediger, Marlow (1990), *"Role of Philosophy in Teaching Science,"* Paideia, 241-246. Published by the Polish Academy of Science, in Warsaw.
7. Ediger Marlow and D. Bhaskara Rao, *Teaching Science Successfully* New Delhi: Discovery Published House.
8. Gardner, Howard (1993), *Multiple Intelligences:* Theory Into Practice. New York: Basic books.
9. National Science Teachers Association (2001), *Classroom Assessment and the National Education Standards.* Washington, DC: the Association, NSTA.
10. Searson, Robert, and Rita Dunn (2001), *"The Learning Style Teaching Model,"* Science and Children, 38 (5), 22-36.

Additional Reading

1. Bhaskara Rao, Digumarti, (1994). *Scientific Aptitude.* New Delhi: Ashish Publishing House.
2. Bhaskara Rao, Digumarti, (1995). *Animal Kingdom.* New Delhi: Discovery Publishing House.
3. Bhaskara Rao, Digumarti, (1995). *Batracology.* New Delhi: Discovery Publishing House.
4. Bhaskara Rao, Digumarti, (1996). *Scientific Attitude vis-a-vis Scientific Aptitude.* New Delhi: Discovery Publishing House.
5. Bhaskara Rao, Digumarti, Editor (1996). *Encyclopedia of Education for All,* 5 Volumes. New Delhi: APH Publishing Corporation.

Vol. I Education for All: The World Conference.

Vol. II Education for All: The EPA-9 Summit.

Vol. III Education for All: Quality Education for All.

Vol. IV Education for All: Planning and Monitoring.

Vol. V Education for All: The Indian Scenario.

6. Bhaskara Rao, Digumarti, Editor (1996). *Global Perceptions on Peace Education,* 3 Volumes. New Delhi: Discovery Publishing House.
7. Bhaskara Rao, Digumarti, Editor (1996). *National Policy on Education,* 2 Volumes. New Delhi: Anmol Publications Pvt. Ltd.
8. Bhaskara Rao, Digumarti, Editor (1997). *Care the Child,* 2 Volumes. New Delhi: Discovery Publishing House.
9. Bhaskara Rao, Digumarti, Editor (1997). *Education for the 21st Century.* New Delhi: Discovery Publishing House.

10. Bhaskara Rao, Digumarti, Editor (1997). *Reflections on Scientific Attitude.* New Delhi: Discovery Publishing House.

11. Bhaskara Rao, Digumarti, Editor (1997). *Scientific Attitude.* New Delhi: Discovery Publishing House.

12. Bhaskara Rao, Digumarti, Editor (1997). *Success Story of a Primary Education Project.* New Delhi: APH Publishing Corporation.

13. Bhaskara Rao, Digumarti, Editor (1997). *World Food Summit.* New Delhi: Discovery Publishing House.

14. Bhaskara Rao, Digumarti, Editor (1998). *Adolescence Education.* New Delhi: Discovery Publishing House.

15. Bhaskara Rao, Digumarti, Editor (1998). *Community and School Nutrition Education.* New Delhi: Discovery Publishing House.

16. Bhaskara Rao, Digumarti, Editor (1998). *District Primary Education Programme.* New Delhi: Discovery Publishing House.

17. Bhaskara Rao, Digumarti, Editor (1998). *Earth Summit,* 2 Volumes. New Delhi: Discovery Publishing House.

18. Bhaskara Rao, Digumarti, Editor (1998). *National Policy on Education: Towards an Enlightened and Humane Society.* New Delhi: Discovery Publishing House.

19. Bhaskara Rao, Digumarti, Editor (1998). *Reforming School Education.* New Delhi: Discovery Publishing House.

20. Bhaskara Rao, Digumarti, Editor (1998). *Teacher Education in India.* New Delhi: Discovery Publishing House.

21. Bhaskara Rao, Digumarti, Editor (1998). *World Summit for Social Development.* New Delhi: Discovery Publishing House.

22. Bhaskara Rao, Digumarti, Editor (2000). *Education for All: Achieving the Goal,* 3 Volumes. New Delhi: APH Publishing Corporation.

Vol. I The Global Consensus.

Vol. II Mid-Decade Review Reports of Regional Seminars.

Vol. III Issues and Trends.

23. Bhaskara Rao, Digumarti, Editor (2000), *International Encyclopedia of AIDS,* 11 Volumes in 13 parts. New Delhi: Discovery Publishing House.

Vol. 1 Introduction to HIV/AIDS.

Vol. 2 HIV/AIDS—Issues and Challenges, 2 parts.

Vol. 3 HIV/AIDS—Socio Economic Realities.

Vol. 5 AIDS and NGOs.

Vol. 6 AIDS and Home Care.

Vol. 7 STD Case Management.

Vol. 8 HIV/AIDS Prevention and Care—Teaching Modules for Nurses and Midwives.

Vol. 9 HIV Prevention Education for Education for Educational Institutions.

Vol. 10. Instructional Modules for AIDS Education.

Vol. 11 School Health Education to prevent AIDS and STD—A Package for Curriculum Planners.

24. Bhaskara Rao, Digumarti, Editor (2000). *International Encyclopaedia of Science and Technology Education,* 10 Volumes. New Delhi: Discovery Publishing House.

Vol. 1 Science and Technology Education.

Vol. 2 Science Education in Developing Countries.

Vol. 3 Organisational Structure of Science.

Vol. 4 Science Education in Asia and the Pacific.

Vol. 5 Science and Technology Education For All.

Vol. 6 Values, Ethics, Talent and Girls in Science and Technology Education.

Vol. 7 Popularisation of Science and Technology Education.

Vol. 8 Science, Power and Society.

Vol. 9 Information Technology.

Vol. 10 Teacher Training in Science and Technology Education

Vol. 11 Science, Technology and Society: A Curriculum Framework.

25. Bhaskara Rao, Digumarti, Editor (2001). *Distance Education in Different Countries.* New Delhi: APH Publishing Corporation.

26. Bhaskara Rao, Digumarti, Editor (2001). *Decentralised Management of Education: Management of Education in Panchayati Raj and Municipal Bodies.* New Delhi: Discovery Publishing House.

27. Bhaskara Rao, Digumarti, Editor (2001). *Electrochemistry for Environmental Protection.* New Delhi: Discovery Publishing House.

28. Bhaskara Rao, Digumarti, Editor (2001). *Global Educational Studies.* New Delhi: Discovery Publishing House.

29. Bhaskara Rao, Digumarti, Editor (2001). *Global Synthesis of Educational Assessment.* New Delhi: Discovery Publishing House.

30. Bhaskara Rao, Digumarti, Editor (2001). *International Encyclopedia of Human Rights,* 7 Volumes in 13 parts. New Delhi: Discovery Publishing House.

Vol. 1 International Instruments of Human Rights, 2 parts.

Vol. 2 Regional Instruments of Human Rights.

Vol. 3 Human Rights and the United Nations, 2 parts.

Vol. 4 Fact Files of Human Rights, 3 parts.

Vol. 5 Study Stories of Human Rights, 3 parts.

Vol. 6 International Meetings on Human Rights, 2 parts.

Vol. 7 Professional Training in Human Rights.

31. Bhaskara Rao, Digumarti, Editor (2001). *Jomtein Decade of Education.* New Delhi: Discovery Publishing House.

32. Bhaskara Rao, Digumarti, Editor (2001). *Nuclear Materials: Issues and Concerns,* 2 Volumes. New Delhi: Discovery Publishing House.

33. Bhaskara Rao, Digumarti, Editor (2001). *World Conference on Education for All.* New Delhi: APH Publishing Corporation.

34. Bhaskara Rao, Digumarti, Editor (2001). *World Conference on Higher Education.* New Delhi: Discovery Publishing House.

35. Bhaskara Rao, Digumarti, Editor (2001). *World Conference on Science.* New Delhi: Discovery Publishing House.

36. Bhaskara Rao, Digumarti, Editor (2003). *Inspairing Experiences in Teacher Education.* New Delhi: Discovery Publishing House.

37. Bhaskara Rao, Digumarti, Editor (2003). *International Studies in Education*, 3 Volumes. New Delhi: Discovery Publishing House.

38. Bhaskara Rao, Digumarti, Editor (2003). *Military Conversion: Impact on Science and Technology*. New Delhi: Discovery Publishing House.

39. Bhaskara Rao, Digumarti, Editor (2003) *United Nations Millennium Summit*. New Delhi: Discovery Publishing House.

40. Bhaskara Rao, Digumarti, Editor (2003). *World Assembly on Aging*. New Delhi: Discovery Publishing House.

41. Bhaskara Rao, Digumarti, Editor (2003). *World Conference on Human Rights*. New Delhi: Discovery Publishing House.

42. Bhaskara Rao, Digumarti, Editor (2003). *World Education Forum*. New Delhi: Discovery Publishing House.

43. Bhaskara Rao, Digumarti, Editor (2003). *Education, Employment and Human Resource Development*. New Delhi: Discovery Publishing House.

44. Bhaskara Rao, Digumarti, Editor (2003). *Learning to Live Together*, 3 Volumes. New Delhi: Discovery Publishing House.

45. Bhaskara Rao, Digumarti, Editor (2003). *Successful Schooling*. New Delhi: Discovery Publishing House.

46. Bhaskara Rao, Digumarti, Editor (2003). *European Education and Teachers*. New Delhi: Discovery Publishing House.

47. Bhaskara Rao, Digumarti, Editor (2003). *Teachers in a Changing World*. New Delhi: Discovery Publishing House.

48. Bhaskara Rao, Digumarti, C.A.P. Swamy & B.S.V. Dutt (1997). *Self Evaluation in Student Teaching*. New Delhi: Discovery Publishing House.

49. Bhaskara Rao, Digumarti & Digumarti Pushpa Latha (1994). *Achievement in Biology*. New Delhi: Discovery Publishing House.

50. Bhaskara Rao, Digumarti C. Sridevei & K. Vijaya (1995). *Achievement in Social Studies*. New Delhi: Discovery Publishing House.

51. Bhaskara Rao, Digumarti & Digumarti Pushpa Latha (1995). *Achievement in English.* New Delhi: Discovery Publishing House.

52. Bhaskara Rao, Digumarti & Digumarti Pushpa Latha (1994). *Achievement in Science.* New Delhi: Discovery Publishing House.

53. Bhaskara Rao, Digumarti & Digumarti Pushpa Latha (1995). *Achievement in Mathematics.* New Delhi: Discovery Publishing House.

54. Bhaskara Rao, Digumarti & Digumarti Pushpa Latha Editors (1998). *International Encyclopaedia of Woman,* 5 Volumes. New Delhi: Discovery Publishing House.

Vol. 1 Status of World's Women.

Vol. 2 Women, Education and Empowerment.

Vol. 3 Women Challenges and Advancement.

Vol. 4 Women and Family Health.

Vol. 5 Women and International Action.

55. Bhaskara Rao, Digumarti & Digumarti Pushpa Latha & Digumarti Harshitha, Editors (2001). *Biological Warfare.* New Delhi: Discovery Publishing House.

56. Bhaskara Rao, Digumarti & Digumarti Pushpa Latha & Digumarthi Harshitha, Editors (2001). *Women as Educators.* New Delhi: Discovery Publishing House.

57. Bhaskara Rao, Digumarti & Digumarti Harshitha, Editors (2001). *Education In India.* New Delhi: APH Publishing Corporation.

58. Bhaskara Rao, Digumarti, Digumarti Pushpa Latha & Digumarthi Harshitha, Editors (2001). *Assessing Learning Achievement.* New Delhi: Discovery Publishing House.

59. Bhaskara Rao, Digumarti, Digurmarti Pushpa Latha & Digumarthi Harshitha, Editors (2001). *Energy Security.* New Delhi: Discovery Publishing House.

60. Bhaskara Rao, Digumarti, D. Harshitha & K.R.S. Sambasiva Rao, Editors (1999). *Advanced Biotechnology.* New Delhi: Discovery Publishing House.

61. Bhaskara Rao, Digumarti & D. Sridhar (2002). *Job Satisfaction of School Teachers.* New Delhi: Discovery Publishing House.

62. Bhaskara Rao, Digumarti & K.R.S. Sambasiva Rao, Editors (1996). *Current Trends in Indian Education.* New Delhi: Discovery Publishing House.

63. Bhaskara Rao, Digumarti & K. Vijya (1995). *A Text Book Evaluation.* Ambala Cantt. The Associated Publishers.

64. Bhaskara Rao, Digumarti & N.V.M. Mohana Rao (2002). *Problems of Mentally Handicapped Children.* New Delhi: Discovery Publishing House.

65. Bhaskara Rao, Digumarti, V.V. Rao, V.V. Lakshmi & V.V. Krishna, Editors (1999)., *Status and Advancement of Women.* New Delhi: APH Publishing Corporation.

66. Babu, P.C. & Digumarti Bhaskara Rao, Editor (2003). *Flowers of Wisdom.* New Delhi: Discovery Publishing House.

67. Bhagya Lakshmi, Lingineni & Digurmarti Bhaskara Rao, Editor (2000). *Reading and Comprehension.* New Delhi: Discovery Publishing House.

68. Bhuvaneswara Lakshmi, Gadde & Digumarti Bhaskara Rao Editor (2000). *Attitude Towards Science.* New Delhi: Discovery Publishing House.

69. Devraj, T.A.S. & Digumarti Bhaskara Rao, Editor (1997). *Trace Analysis of Uranium and Thorium.* New Delhi: Discovery Publishing House.

70. Durga Rani, K. & Digumarthi Bhaskara Rao, Editor (2000). *Educational Aspirations and Scientific Attitudes.* New Delhi: Discovery Publishing House.

71. Dutt, B.S.V. & Digumarti Bhaskara Rao (2001). *Empowering Primary Teachers.* New Delhi: Discovery Publishing House.

72. Ediger, Marlow & Digumarti Bhaskara Rao (1996). *Science Curriculum.* New Delhi: Discovery Publishing House.

73. Ediger, Marlow & Digumarti Bhaskara Rao (2000). *Teaching Mathematics Successfully.* New Delhi: Discovery Publishing House.

74. Ediger, Marlow & Digumarti Bhaskara Rao (2001). *Teaching Science Successfully.* New Delhi: Discovery Publishing House.

75. Ediger, Marlow & Digumarti Bhaskara Rao (2001). *Teaching Social Studies Successfully*. New Delhi: Discovery Publishing House.

76. Ediger, Marlow & Digumarti Bhaskara Rao (2002), *Philosophy and Curriculum*. New Delhi: Discovery Publishing House.

77. Ediger, Marlow & Digumarti Bhaskara Rao (2003). *Psychology and Curriculum*. New Delhi: Discovery Publishing House.

78. Ediger, Marlow & Digumarti Bhaskara Rao (2003). *Improving School Administration*. New Delhi: Discovery Publishing House.

79. Ediger, Marlow & Digumarti Bhaskara Rao (2003). *Elementary Curriculum*. New Delhi: Discovery Publishing House.

80. Ediger, Marlow & Digumarti Bhaskara Rao (2003). *Language Arts Curriculum*. New Delhi: Discovery Publishing House.

81. Ediger, Marlow & Digumarti Bhaskara Rao (2003). *Teaching Language Arts Successfully*. New Delhi: Discovery Publishing House.

82. Ediger, Marlow & Digumarti Bhaskara Rao (2003). *Teaching Mathematics in Elementary Schools*. New Delhi: Discovery Publishing House.

83. Ediger, Marlow & Digumarti Bhaskara Rao (2003). *Teaching Science in Elementary Schools*. New Delhi: Discovery Publishing House.

84. Ediger, Marlow & Digumarti Bhaskara Rao (2003). *Teaching Social Studies in Elementary School*. New Delhi: Discovery Publishing House.

85. Ediger, Marlow, B.S.V. Dutt & Digumarti Bhaskara Rao (2003), *Teaching English Successfully*, New Delhi: Discovery Publishing House.

86. Jayasree, Kandi & Digumarti Bhaskara Rao, Editor (1999). *Correlates of Socialisation*. New Delhi: Discovery Publishing House.

87. John Babu, Ch. & T.J.R. Prasad, G.M. Madhukar an Digumarti Bhaskara Rao, Editors (1996). *Problem Solving in Mathematics*. New Delhi: APH Publishing Corporation.

88. Jyothi, Nirmala & Digumarti Bhaskara Rao, Editor (2003). *Non-detention System in School Education.* New Delhi: Discovery Publishing House.

89. Majra, Talvi & Digumarti Bhaskara Rao, Editors (1996). *Educational Leadership and Social Changes.* New Delhi: Discovery Publishing House.

90. Prabhakaram, K.S. & Digumarti Bhaskara Rao, Editors (1998). *Concept Attainment Model in Mathematics Teaching.* New Delhi: Discovery Publishing House.

91. Prasanth Kumar, J. & Digumarti Bhaskara Rao, Editor (1998). *Effectiveness of Distance Education System.* New Delhi: Discovery Publishing House.

92. Prasanth Kumar, U. & Digumarti Bhaskara Rao, and G. Sundara Rao, Editors (2000). *Open University—Student Support Services.* New Delhi: Discovery Publishing House.

93. Ramatulasamma, K. & Digumarti Bhaskara Rao, Editor (2003). *Job Satisfaction of Teacher Educators.* New Delhi: Discovery Publishing House.

94. Ramakrishnaiah, D. & Digumarti Bhaskara Rao, Editor (1998). *Job Satisfaction of College Teachers.* New Delhi: Discovery Publishing House.

95. Rathaiah, Lavu & Digumarti Bhaskara Rao, Editor (1996), *International Innovations in Education.* New Delhi: Discovery Publishing House.

96. Rathaiah, Lavu & Digumarti Bhaskara Rao, (1997). *Achievement Correlates.* New Delhi: Discovery Publishing House.

97. Ramesh, Ganta & Digumarti Bhaskara Rao, Editor (1998). *Environmental Education: Problems and Prospects.* New Delhi: Discovery Publishing House.

98. Reddy, Sudhakar & Digumarti Bhaskara Rao. Editor (2003). *Creativity in Adolescents.* New Delhi: Discovery Publishing House.

99. Reddy, M.S. & Digumarti Bhaskara Rao, Editor (2003). *Creativity in College Students.* New Delhi: Discovery Publishing House.

100. Rudramamba, B. & Digumarti Bhaskara Rao, Editor (2003). *Impact of the Problems of Teachers on Achievement of Pupils.* New Delhi: APH Publishing Corporation.

101. Sanjeeva Rao, P.C. & Digumarti Bhaskara Rao, Editor (1996). *A Text Book of Geology.* New Delhi: Discovery Publishing House.

102. Satya Narayana, V. & Digumarti Bhaskara Rao, Editor (2001). *Physical Education, Social Attitudes and Leadership Qualities.* New Delhi: Discovery Publishing House.

103. Srinivasulu Reddy, M., K.R.S. Sambasiva Rao & Digumarti Bhaskara Rao, Editor (1999). *A Text Book of Aquaculture.* New Delhi: Discovery Publishing House.

104. Srinivasa Rao, M. & Digumarti Bhaskara Rao, Editor (2003). *Achievement Motivation and Achievement in Mathematics.* New Delhi: Discovery Publishing House.

105. Vanaja, M. & Digumarti Bhaskara Rao, Editor (1999). *Inquiry Training Model.* New Delhi: Discovery Publishing House.

106. Valeri V. Koustiouk & Digumarti Bhaskara Rao, Editor (2003). *A Text Book of Cryogenics.* New Delhi: Discovery Publishing House.

107. Veena Kumari, Balusu & Digumarti Bhaskara Rao, (1996). *Operation Black Board.* New Delhi: Ashish Publishing House.

108. Veena Kumari, Balusu & Digumarti Bhaskara Rao, Editor (2000). *Psycho-Social Correlates of Achievement.* New Delhi: Discovery Publishing House.

109. Venkata Rao, P. & Digumarti Bhaskara Rao, (1998). *A Text Book of Zoology—Junior Intermediate.* Guntur: Vignan Publishers.

110. Venkata Rao, P. & Digumarti Bhaskara Rao, Editor (1989). *A Text Book of Zoology—Senior Intermediate.* Guntur: Vignan Publishers.

111. Venugopala Rao, K. & Digumarti Bhaskara Rao, Editor (2000). *Teacher Morale in Secondary Schools.* New Delhi: Discovery Publishing House.

112. Vidya, C. & Digumarti Bhaskara Rao, Editor (1996). *A Text Book of Nutrition.* New Delhi: Discovery Publishing House.

113. Vidya Bharathi, D. & Digumarti Bhaskara Rao, Editor (2000). *Educational Philosophies of Swami Vivekanand and John Dewey.* New Delhi: APH Publishing Corporation.

114. Vidya, C. & Digumarti Bhaskara Rao, Editor (1996). *A Text Book of Nutrition.* New Delhi: Discovery Publishing House.

115. Bhaskara Rao, Digumarti (1986). *Dhrushya Sravana Bodhanapakaranalu* (Audio Visual Teaching Aids). Guntur: Nagarjuna Publishers.

116. Bhaskara Rao, Digumarti (1993). *Jeevasashtra Bodhana* (Teaching of Biology). Guntur: Nagarjuna Publishers.

117. Bhaskara Rao, Digumarti (1995). *Vignanasasthra Bodhana* (Teaching of science). Guntur: Nagarjuna Publishers.

118. Bhaskara Rao, Digumarti (1997). *Vidya Manovignana Seshtram* (Educational Psychology). Guntur: Creative Press.

119. Bhaskara Rao, Digumarti (1998). *DSC Study Material.* Guntur: Nagarjuna Publishers.

120. Bhaskara Rao, Digumarti. (1998). *Upadhyayudu Vidya* (Teacher and Education). Guntur: Nagarjuna Publishers.

121. Bhaskara Rao, Digumarti (1998). *Vidya Drukpadalu* (Perspectives of Education). Guntur: Nagarjuna Publishers.

122. Bhaskara Rao, Digumarti (1999). *EDCET Teaching Aptitude.* Guntur: Nagarjuna Publishers.

123. Bhaskara Rao, Digumarti (2001). *Bharata Samajamulo Upadyayudu Vidya* (Teacher and Education in Emerging Indian Society). Guntur: Nagarjuna Publishers.

124. Bhaskara Rao, Digumarti (2001). *Bhoutiks Sastra Bodhana Paddathulu* (Methods of Teaching Physical Science). Guntur: Nagarjuna Publishers.

125. Bhaskara Rao, Digumarti (2001). *Jeeva Sastra Bodhana Padhathulu* (Methods of Teaching Biology). Guntur: Nagarjuna Publishers.

126. Bhaskara Rao, Digumarti (2001). *Vidya Manovignana Sastram* (Educational Psychology). Guntur: Nagarjuna Publishers.

127. Bhaskara Rao, Digumarti (2003). *Patasala Yajamanyam Paripalana* (School Management and Administration). Guntur: Nagarjuna Publishers.

128. Bhaskara Rao, Digumarti (2003). *Vidya Sanketika Sastram Mariyu Computer Vidya* (Educational Technology and Computer Education). Guntur: Nagarjuna Publishers.

Index